Your Way with God's Word

Your Way with God's Word

■ Discovering Your Distinctive ■
Preaching Voice

David J. Schlafer

COWLEY PUBLICATIONS
Cambridge ✦ Boston
Massachusetts

Published in the United States of America by Cowley Publications, a division of the Society of St. John
the Evangelist. No portion of this book may be reproduced, stored in or introduced into a retrieval
system, or transmitted, in any form or by any means—including photocopying—without the prior
written permission of Cowley Publications, except in the case of brief quotations embodied in critical
articles and reviews.

Library of Congress Cataloging-in-Publication Data:
Schlafer, David J., 1944–
Your way with God's word: discovering your distinctive preaching voice /
David J. Schlafer
p.   cm.
ISBN 1-56101-118-5 (alk. paper)
1. Preaching. 2. Public speaking—Religious aspects—Christianity. I. Title.
BV4211.2.S365   1995
251—dc20   95-21264 CIP

Editor: Cynthia Shattuck
Copyeditor and Designer: Vicki Black

This book is printed on recycled, acid-free paper and was produced in the United States of America.

Cowley Publications
28 Temple Place
Boston, Massachusetts 02111

For Peggy,
who demonstrates with eloquence
that "silence is fullness"

Table of Contents

Part III
Toward a Homiletical Spirituality

Acknowledgments

I am deeply grateful to...

Celinda Hughes of Cokesbury Seminars, for seeding the vision that eventually grew into this book by inviting me to present a seminar on "Naming and Claiming Your Distinctive Preaching Voice" at Proclamation 94 in Nashville, Tennessee.

The College of Preachers; its Warden, the Rev. Canon Erica Wood, for the privilege of serving as Interim Director of Studies throughout the writing process; and especially Ruth Frey and Shelagh Casey Brown, treasured colleagues during my time at the College.

Dean Martha Horne and Professor Judith McDaniel for their collegial support during my concurrent appointment as Adjunct Professor of Homiletics at Virginia Theological Seminary; and members of my homiletics classes at VTS, who helped me test materials contained here and who, rather than simply being homiletics students, entered without inhibition into the risky venture of becoming preaching colleagues.

Clergy and lay preachers in the Episcopal dioceses of Chicago, California, Wyoming, Oregon, Louisiana, and Oklahoma, who undertook this adventure of homiletical self-discernment in retreat and workshop settings.

Donna Osthaus, Susan Gaumer, O. C. Edwards, G. Porter Taylor, Joyce Glover, Gail Jones, Kristen Schlafer, and Margaret Tucker, who perused the manuscript from start to finish and offered careful, encouraging commentary.

The Rev. Molly Doreza and the Rev. Joy Rogers for permission to use their sermons.

Cynthia Shattuck and Vicki Black, editors *par excellence* at Cowley Publications, for seeing the possibilities and negotiating the technical hurdles in a project of this sort.

Introduction

Different Ways to Undertake the Adventure

This book invites you to explore the riches of your preaching voice: how it is unique, how it is informed by the voices of others, how it can be orchestrated with other preaching voices in celebrating what no single voice can adequately convey.

There are many ways to undertake this adventure. Some of the routes suggested below may strike you as more engaging than others. By all means take the fork in the road that is most intriguing! Peruse the other possibilities, however. Paths that are well suited to your present purposes may differ from those that will best serve your preaching needs and interests down the track.

1. For the General Homiletical Development of Individual Preachers

You may be primarily concerned to take advantage of your own preaching resources—resources that are ready-to-hand but easier to employ if they are clearly named and carefully reflected upon. If that is the case, you may wish to use this book as a journal for a professional retreat. The retreat could take the form of:

■ *An extended, concentrated period of reflection,* where you go off by yourself for a few days, free from your regular routine and from the telephone. At your own pace, you can ponder the most relevant questions in each chapter of Part II (while walking, or with your feet propped up). Be sure to give yourself plenty of time for each chapter. Make notes as you go along, or at the conclusion of each stage of reflection. Allow for significant "break" time (including rest, recreation, and prayer space) between each chapter. Spend time in summary reflection at the conclusion of the retreat, asking yourself what you have learned about the preacher you are, and how that learning might be manifested in sermons you will preach in the weeks ahead.

■ *A planned, periodic commitment to personal growth,* in which you undertake the retreat process one chapter at a time, one week (or month) at a time. In this format it is important to designate a safe space to which you return in a regular rhythm. Those familiar with the Spiritual Exercises of Ignatius Loyola will recognize the parallels between a standard retreat of given duration, and an "Annotation 19" retreat, which is adapted for the daily use of those who cannot leave their regular responsibilities to spend full time in reflection.

2. For the Professional Growth of a Small Group of Preachers

Given the "preaching as a sacred conversation" theme developed in this book, it would be ideal to undertake the process outlined above in the company of a select group of preaching companions, where each can support and be supported by other members of the group. Such a shared venture could be taken in two ways:

■ *On an extended group retreat,* perhaps with the facilitating services of another preacher, skilled lay listener, or teacher of preaching.

■ *At a regular gathering to which all preaching colleagues commit,* where the agenda for the meeting is reserved for the shared exploration of preaching voices.

In both options, individual as well as group time is essential. In the second option, individual work needs to be done prior to meetings of the group.

3. For Developing the Mutual Ministry of Clergy and Lay Preachers

The preaching conversation, if it is healthy, is not held in "executive session," where attendance is restricted to the "professionals." Others who share in the conversation can also use this book to explore their preaching voices:

■ *Clergy and lay leaders together.* Appropriate refinements could be made in the exercises for laypersons whose ministry of proclamation usually takes place between Monday and Saturday, and beyond the walls of the church building.

■ *Lay leaders only.* All lay leaders who are interested in discerning and developing their own ministries of proclamation can participate. The group could include but should not be restricted to those licensed to preach at Sunday services. The focus here is to understand "preaching" and "preachers" in their most inclusive and fundamental sense.

4. In a Religious Institutional Setting

The exercises of this book thrive in contexts that are independent of official ecclesiastical sanction. That doesn't mean, however, that those operating "within the system" are excluded from sharing in the fun! These materials can be employed in:

■ *Clergy conferences and continuing education programs on preaching.* The basic design of the book was initially shaped for a continuing education program, and various versions of the exercises have been "field tested" in a number of clergy conferences. Even when time and space have been limited, these gatherings have been characterized by high energy, vulnerability, and candor, as preachers have been invited to reflect upon and share dimensions of their preaching journeys with colleagues, some of whom they have scarcely known. This book can be used either as the single focus of a retreat, conference, or workshop, or as a significant segment in program design focused more broadly on the preaching task. I am delighted either to offer or to receive suggestions for use of this material in such settings.

■ *Seminary courses in homiletics.* I have found that if I start preaching classes with "The Principles," student preachers tend to struggle inefficiently as they try to "measure up" to an assumed "sermon ideal" which is, in fact, an abstract fiction. On the other hand, given the space to consider their distinctive characteristics not as weeds to be pulled out but as seeds to nurture, fledgling preachers undertake "the basics" with zest and insight concerning how principles of preaching take fresh form in their own particular cases.

5. In Preparation for Specific Sermons

While the primary value of these exercises may be in "soft-focus," broad-sweep preaching preparation, the methods can also be used as a part of specific preparation for particular preaching events:

■ *When a connection between sermon content and preacher's experience is already evident.* Sometimes a resonance between Scripture text, congregational need, cultural situation, or liturgical requirement and a particular aspect of your preaching voice is apparent. If that is the case, then preparation for the sermon involves an exploration of that dimension in your experience. You do not have to take the full measure of your preaching life in order to explore any particular aspect.

■ *When a "block" is encountered in sermon preparation.* When the study of Scripture seems to take you nowhere, or when you seem to get seriously "stuck," it may be helpful to scan the "points" on the map introduced in chapter 3. Ask yourself which places evoke special energy. On several occasions, I have found that Scripture text, preaching context, and long-forgotten life experience suddenly "click" when this preparation procedure is observed. It does not necessarily follow (in fact, it seldom does) that I use the life experience in the sermon itself, either named as such or indirectly employed. Rather, a fresh window on the text is suggested, as fresh light is shed on my experience. Sermon "blocks" are not necessarily occasioned by unacknowledged sins, shames, or wounds. Frequently the message is: "Pay attention! You have a special insight to offer out of a significant achievement or a deep joy—but only if you will sit long enough for the connection to reveal itself."

6. As One Dimension in Systematic
Sermon Review and Assessment

The categories, or way stations, on this homiletical journey can be used as:

■ *Points of tracking* for revisiting a sermon recently delivered, as you look and listen for how the preacher was disclosed in the sermon.

■ *Springboards for reflection* in a broad survey of sermon patterns. Every once in a while, preachers need to step back and take stock of the broad trajectory of their sermons. What are the axes you are grinding? What are blind spots which (by their very nature) you have been missing? Seeing what you have shared more than enough of, what you have been oblivious to, what you have recently discovered but not yet incorporated, can be very instructive.

7. As a Centering Point for
Developing Your Homiletical Spirituality

For many preachers, spiritual growth and health are intimately tied to their preaching ministries. These preachers are not necessarily more accomplished in their preaching, or more mature in their relationship with God just because preaching is so critical for them. It is simply that preaching is particularly close to the heart of who God is calling them to be.

If that is the case for you, the dimensions of life experience posed for homiletical reflection in this book can serve as primary focal points for discernment and spiritual direction as well. Ongoing attention in these areas can be incorporated into a systematic life of prayer, and offered to others with whom you are in a covenant and share some degree of spiritual intimacy. In conjunction with self-examination, support group process, or spiritual direction, materials discovered in the journey mapped out in these pages can be prayerfully reflected upon.

8. As a Starting Point for
Developing a Theology of Preaching

All of the preceding suggested uses of this book focus on the process of exploration contained in Part II. Parts I and III sketch out an interplay of concepts and metaphors that hint at the mystery of what a preacher is up to when he or she undertakes the audacity of preaching.

I envisioned this book as a diagnostic device for individual preachers to use in discovering how they are unique. The more I have worked on it, however, the more its "sacred speech community" theme has worked on me. Without a nurturing community, no speech would ever emerge. Without a faith community and a company of preaching colleagues—some in direct contact, others cheering us on from their vantage point in the "great cloud of witnesses" described in Hebrews 11—preaching would have no point, and would not be.

"Preaching is a sacred conversation" is the truth that has formed itself in the center of my imagination as I have lived with this book during its writing. I have come to believe that it is an essential starting point in any theology of preaching. Perhaps, reflecting on that metaphor, you also will be led to some insights concerning the nature of preaching—insights metaphorical or conceptual, artistic or systematic. If so, I trust you will celebrate and share them among the company of preachers with whom you are privileged to listen and to speak.

9. As an Occasion for Homiletical Free Play

All these suggested patterns may just seem like so much work to do. You may simply want to read the book—and perhaps even fill some of the abundant white spaces with homiletical doodles, or cartoons of preachers you have known. If that's what works for you, go right ahead! There are innumerable ways to undertake this adventure: the only essential thing is to start the journey.

Part I

Finding Your Voice as a Preacher

■ 1 ■

How Do You Sound in Your Sermons?

Preachers tend to grit their teeth the first few times they have to hear a recording or see a videotape of their own sermons: "I can't believe I look so dumb!" "Am I really that boring?" The reaction is not surprising: it *is* a bit of a shock for most of us to see and hear ourselves the way that others see and hear us. Still, the intensity of these negative reactions is a bit of a puzzle, isn't it? After all, most people are used to looking at pictures of themselves. They even line up to pose for them. Making tapes—audio tapes or videotapes—is not a novel procedure. Lots of people record themselves and find it fascinating to review the results—often over and over again.

So why the high anxiety over preaching tapes? Perhaps it is because the tape of a sermon records a solo performance. We often become more self-conscious than usual when we know that the eyes and ears of others are fixed on us alone. With a sermon, however, that solo performance takes place when the sermon is preached. For better or worse, when the event is over, it's *over*. What is so hard about revisiting the occasion, after the fact? Many preachers won't even watch or listen to their sermon tapes in private, and if they do manage to steel themselves to confront the ordeal, the anticipatory angst and subsequent chagrin seem, if not beyond all reason, at least out of all proportion. What is there about hearing and seeing ourselves preach that so many of us find so unnerving?

Preacher John Claypool may help us get a bearing on this question. Actors, he observes, are "on stage" in their performances but they normally interpret texts composed by other people. Authors present material that comes from their own experience, yet the words they write are encountered by readers in a setting from which the author is usually absent. For both author and actor, therefore, "safe spaces" separate speaker, message, and hearer. In a sermon, however, the preacher presents personal material directly. In preaching, Claypool notes, the sense of intimacy is inevitable. For many public speakers, the task of standing before a group of people to communicate something "in their own words" generates a terror that approaches claustrophobia—and preachers have a far heavier responsibility than other speakers.

Preachers are expected not simply to read Scripture or to parrot words that someone else has come up with, but to present fresh and engaging ideas of their own. At the same time, they are not free to say whatever comes to mind, or to express just any conviction they happen to hold. Preachers are expected to offer *God's* word in *their own* words. So perhaps the sense of anxiety preachers have about revisiting such a daunting experience through the tape of their sermons is intelligible after all!

To take preaching with any seriousness is a tall order. Conscientious preachers labor long hours over what they will say. Then they do the best they can to deliver what they have prepared. The preaching process is arduous; the experience may be difficult, even painful. It is always energy draining, even if it comes off all right. Why should any preacher have to endure a replay of such a vulnerable moment? That is asking a lot!

Yet the psychological dynamic is seldom one of antipathy, pure and simple. There is also a certain lure—an attraction we preachers have to watching the replay that we would rather not see. Reticent though we may be, we are curious all the same. I *would* like to have some sense of how my sermon really went. If the answer is "Very well indeed," it would be nice to know that. Perhaps, after a sigh of relief and a cautious flow of humble satisfaction, I will be able to convince myself that the next sermon won't be quite so daunting. After all, who needs a weekly ball and chain of needless worry?

Besides that, there might be something I can learn from watching and listening to myself. No matter how good my preaching is, surely there is room for growth. What better way to improve my preaching than to observe it in the very act, rather than relying on my receding memory and the vague compliments parishioners offer as they shake my hand at the back door of the church on Sunday morning?

That's what my mind says, but somehow my body still shrinks from the prospect of actually sitting down before the tape-player or the VCR. "Perhaps I'll listen to my sermon later, when I have a bit more objectivity," I tell myself. "Besides, pastoral calls and paperwork have been piling up over the weekend while I was trying to get my sermon up to speed...."

My inhibitions, however, may be more than psychological. There are solid theological reasons that can be mustered to stay my hand from punching the "play" button on my tape deck. Let's consider a couple of the more obvious ones.

Preaching is not supposed to be a variation on a beauty contest. Preachers who are out on stage simply to strut their homiletical stuff have no business in the pulpit. Priestly preaching or prophetic preaching—it makes no difference. The preacher is not the one to be in focus. Priests and prophets alike have this in common: they are representatives, message mediators, icons of God. Preoccupation with one's own preaching can easily become idolatrous. If a preacher, with finite resources in finite time, prepares as faithfully as possible, then it is not only right but essential to leave the rest to God, rather than to obsess about the result.

God's word, the Scriptures promise, will not return empty. God's power is not dependent upon how well we perform. Even the best-laid sermon plans sometimes come unraveled; on the other hand, our seeming sermon failures sometimes fuel holy fires in the hearts of those who hear them. God is not above using sermons that are inept, irresponsible, or even outright rebellious. In the last analysis, the results of our preaching are none of our business. To try to make them so is not just useless; it is sin. That is one very good reason why we may have cause for pause before uncritically appropriating the readily available fruit of modern communication technology. That fruit might just be a contemporary offspring of the "apple" plucked from Eden's tree.

Another possible objection to spending time with a sermon tape is a practical consideration that is related to but different from the first objection. Sermon preparation is an enormous undertaking. If seminary training teaches preachers anything, it is that we cannot responsibly preach without doing a mountain of homework. "An hour in the study for every moment in the pulpit" is the often-propagated rule of thumb. The ideal checklist of tasks to be accomplished in a single sermon venture is staggering, and only the most seasoned preacher has a chance of getting through that list, even if shaping sermons were the only responsibility a pastor had!

Reflective, responsible preachers know very well before going into their sermons how much they have left undone, how little time they have had to unearth, integrate, and polish. They are keenly aware that they did not preach the perfect sermon last Sunday, regardless of how warm and widespread were the post-service accolades from grateful listeners. A quick review of the manuscript or the sermon notes will be quite enough to refresh their memories as to what they didn't come close to getting right—or even getting around to. So what is the point of an extended post-mortem? Next Sunday's sermon won't be perfect either, but unlike last Sunday's sermon, it hasn't been written yet. If there is something obvious to be learned from last week, it needs to be picked up en route to *next* week.

The results of our preaching, then, are not our business, and the responsibilities of preaching are always in the future. The combined thrust of these two points is clear: the sermon is not about the preacher, but an offering of nurture from the gospel. It is altogether appropriate to focus our attention upon the hungry people whom God loves, and the food with which God wants to feed them. Concerns about our sermons need to be focused primarily on the act of preparing nourishment, and on the methods we use that directly facilitate this end. Fixations on technique, style, "pulpit presence," or preaching reputation are out of place.

With these theological objections in mind, it is not hard to guess why preachers are so reticent to watch "instant replays" of their preaching, since that is not "where the action is." Yet the same haunting questions remain: How do I sound in the sermon? What is my way with God's word? No matter how frequently or rigorously we set them aside, and no matter how ambivalent we feel when we catch sight of them out of the corners of our eyes, these questions won't go away. Or, if they do, they don't stay put. They depart for a time, and sneak back in to tempt us unexpectedly at moments of greater vulnerability.

Perhaps we cannot exorcise the questions because, even as preachers, we are creatures of our own culture. It is hard to imagine, say, Thomas Aquinas, or even John Wesley giving much thought to these issues. Surely they worked on their sermons and tried to learn from their experiences of preaching. Maybe they fretted occasionally if their sermons did not seem to hang together or to gain a receptive hearing. But to envision Aquinas or Wesley going on and on about their own preaching voices just doesn't compute. Such preoccupations were not important to their culture. With us it is otherwise. Ours is an age of self-preoccupation. We watch ourselves doing practically everything, and worry a great deal about what we see.

Preachers, after all, are human. To be a human being is inevitably to be caught up in the currents of one's own cultural experience. We may have some perspective on these underlying concerns, but we are swept along in them all the same. Until society moves on to other fixations, preachers are likely to be stuck with these approach/avoidance visits to the homiletical hall of mirrors.

If that is the situation, how shall we deal with it? One possible approach is, "If you can't beat it, join it." A deliberate commitment to homiletical self-reflection is a very good thing, say those who find this approach congenial. The gospel is about the Incarnation, and without careful, ongoing attention to the person of the preacher, the "gospel" that is preached will be abstract and disembodied. If the incarnate preacher is absent from the preaching event, all talk of Incarnation will have a hollow ring. The medium and the message will be radically out of sync unless preachers pay attention to the distinctive persons that they are, and how the person is an active presence in the preaching process. In brief: if the most careful consideration is not given to *your way* with God's word, this word will come across as flat and unappetizing.

Another possible approach comes from the opposite direction: "If you can't completely overcome homiletical self-consciousness, at least you can give it a good fight." An essential element in Christian preaching, urge advocates of this position, is a critique of the whole enterprise of self-absorption. The gospel diagnoses it as a spiritual disease, and provides a liberating prescription against the cultural narcissism typically revealed in questions of "What kind of a preacher am I?" All flesh is grass; not only do all human idiosyncrasies wither, they are not very interesting after a while. If the most careful consideration is not given to your way with *God's* word, then *your* word will not be worth listening to.

As a preacher myself, one who has been richly nourished by the preaching of many different voices and who finds deep joy in helping others learn to preach, I feel keenly the competing attractions of both perspectives. Time and again I have been left high and dry, empty and starved, by preachers who might as well have been the computerized, mechanical voices you hear in voice mail and on long, motorized passageways at airline terminals in major cities. I have also been thoroughly disgusted (that is not too strong a term) by preachers who have seemed, consciously or unconsciously, to be so full of themselves that they were all but incapable of feeding their congregations anything else.

"Living with the tension" between these two perspectives is easier said than done. But trying to work that tension out—in ways that are common to all preachers yet unique to each one—is what we are about in this book.

In all that follows, I do not intend to equate "preacher" and "ordained clergy." In fact, exactly the opposite. In my first book, *Surviving the Sermon: A Guide to Preaching for Those Who Have to Listen*, I argued that the preaching ministry is the responsibility of the entire Christian community and that good sermon listeners are always active participants at every stage in the preaching process. Lay ministers have not only a stake, but a share in the preaching event. Their participation in preaching may well lead many lay ministers to more or less formal preaching opportunities of their own. So the journey for which this book presents a suggested map is their journey too.

"Preaching" also has a still wider connotation that is critical to Christian faith and life. All Christians, by their baptism, are commissioned to "proclaim by word and example the Good News of God in Christ." The most effective "sermons" are often those that come out of the struggle and the dance of daily life, proclaimed by those who would never dream of regarding themselves as "preachers." I hope that this book can be for them as well a means of more deeply discerning their gifts and graces for ministry—which, at its heart, is also a ministry of proclamation.

What does it mean to find and form, to shape and share one's own distinctive preaching voice? How does one undertake such an adventure? Let us see what we can discover.

■ 2 ■

Your Place in the Sacred Conversation

Minutes before the start of a preaching class, one of its members rushed into my office out of breath and out of sorts. "I can't come to class today," he said. I could not believe what I was hearing. This young man had never missed class before. He had heretofore impressed me as a solid student. He was not obviously ill. And he was "up" that day—scheduled as one of the preachers for the class that was about to convene. My mind leaped to angry conclusions: he hadn't done his homework. He was going to offer some lame explanation for an unfinished sermon. A stern professional rebuke gathered itself in my head.

"My daughter just got sick," he said. "My wife can't leave work to come home and stay with her." Now a look of frustration crossed his eyes as he glanced down. My eyes followed his. He had not come into my office empty-handed.

"I really wanted to deliver this sermon today," he said, putting a fully prepared manuscript on my desk. "I've worked very hard on it, and I was looking forward to talking about it with the class, along with the other sermons. I know how important it is for all of us to be involved in this process together."

"Thank you for bringing it over," I said, ashamed at my hasty conclusions. "The least I can do is take it along to class. I'll present it for you. Everyone can talk about it, and we'll incorporate it into our discussions of the other sermons. I know that isn't nearly as good as your being there to deliver it yourself, but you and I can review the sermon together after your daughter gets better. That way all of us will benefit from the work you have done." Visibly relieved, he thanked me and left.

Chastened, I took his sermon text along and did as I had promised. He had produced a sermon that positively sparkled. I delivered his sermon with energy and care. When I finished reading it, the class sat in silence for quite some time. "It doesn't work," someone finally said. "The sermon is very good, but it doesn't fit. That was George's sermon. It sounds like George. It doesn't work the same when you try to preach it."

Everyone else promptly agreed. George and I could no more trade sermons than we could have traded signatures or fingerprints. We had different preaching "voices." So do each of us. I would never have seen the fact so clearly if I had not experienced it so vividly.

A "preaching signature" is probably a better way of trying to illustrate what I mean by "preaching voice" than "preaching fingerprints." Your fingerprints were fixed before your birth. While your fingerprints do get bigger as your body grows, the characteristic pattern they display never alters in the least. Your preaching voice is not like that. Like your handwriting, your preaching voice does develop and modify over time. Like your signature, your actual preaching pattern may also vary a good deal from one situation to another, depending on a number of different conditions under which you do your preaching, such as different types of Scripture texts, different congregational dynamics, different pastoral situations, different levels of expertise you have in different subject matters, different moods and personal circumstances in the midst of which you prepare your sermons.

Once discerned, however, the distinctiveness of your preaching voice can be *recognized* even if, like your handwriting, it cannot always be *described* or sometimes even *understood*. Different people write very differently even when they are writing the same words. Different people also preach differently, even when they are using similar stories, ideas, and images to celebrate the same Word. There can be, therefore, no "ideal sermon" that every preacher should attempt to approximate, just as there can be no "perfect signature," no perfect painting, symphony, poem, or personal relationship.

It may be worth our while to have another look at parallels between your signature and your preaching voice. It would be a serious mistake to claim that, since your handwriting and your preaching are both unique, it is therefore useless for anybody else to give you training in them—either in how to get started, or in how to get better. Both handwriting and preaching can be learned, improved upon, and, in a certain, limited sense, even taught.

The principles of handwriting or preaching, however, cannot function as boiler plates. To the extent that abstract rules are imposed upon a person's handwriting or preaching, the learning process will be very frustrating. The finished products may be neat, correct, or smooth; in the end, however, the writing or the preaching will be lacking in life. Mass-produced mechanical counterfeits of personal signatures are not signatures. Clones of preaching giants are not great preachers. If there is anything more deadly than a prefabricated sermon, it is an ever-so-efficient, ever-so-predictable preacher.

The issues we are wrestling with here were given eloquent expression many years ago by Phillips Brooks, rector of Trinity Church, Boston, and Bishop of Massachusetts, in his classic *Lectures on Preaching,*[1] written at a time when the preaching voices of women were seldom heard:

> Preaching is the communication of truth by man to men. It has in it two essential elements, truth and personality. Neither of those can it spare, and still be preaching. The truest truth, the most authoritative statement of God's will, communicated in any other way than through the personality of brother man to men is not preached truth. (5)

> Christianity is Christ; and we can easily understand how a truth which is of such peculiar character that a person who can stand forth and say of it, "I am the truth," must always be best conveyed through, must indeed be almost incapable of being perfectly conveyed except through personality. (7)

> The truth must come really through the person, not merely over his lips, not merely into his understanding and out through his pen. It must come through his character, his affections, his whole intellectual and moral being. It must generally come through him. (9)

The power of Brooks's position is felt today, I suspect, both in the eloquence of its phrasing and in the exclusivity of its gender focus. Just as my class was the poorer because my student could not be present to deliver his own sermon, the church has been impoverished by the exclusion of women (and those who have been socially marginalized) from the preaching office.

Unfortunately, however, the much-quoted definition "Preaching is truth through personality" has been used as a license, or even an injunction, for preachers to let their warts and wounds and weirdnesses "all hang out." The maxims "Be attentive to Scripture," "Be rooted in Christian history and doctrine," "Be faithful to the gospel," and "Be sensitive to the needs of your congregation" are swept aside by some preachers in favor of something simpler: "Be yourself!" Brooks, in fact, explicitly counters this misrepresentation:

> There are some preachers to whom one might listen for a year, and then he could write their biography, if that were worth the doing. Every truth they wish to teach is illustrated by some event in their own history. Every change of character they wish to urge is set forth under the form in which that change took place in them....It is the crudest attempt to blend personality and truth. They are not fused to one another, but only tied together. (116-117)

> In parishes where such strong prominence belongs to the preacher's personality, where people are always hearing of how he learned this truth or passed through that emotion, all apprehension of thought and realization of experience narrows itself....The rich variety and largeness of the Christian life is lost....Every parishioner is a weakened repetition of the minister's ideas and ways. (118)

The problem here is akin to that over which one stumbles in any sort of one-sided indulgence. The "personality" thus pandered produces results that are every bit as monolithic as those of any abstract "ideal sermon." Boiler plates are boiler plates.

Returning once more to the signature analogy, if a person's signature is so idiosyncratic as to be unintelligible, it is wasted work. A signature is essentially pointless if nobody can make out the letters in it. If all our listeners can say after listening to us preach is "My, what a distinctive voice you have!" then what has been delivered is not an effective sermon—not the living, personal word of God, but a tale told by an idiot, as Shakespeare would say, or a noisy gong or clanging cymbal, to quote St. Paul.

So how do we go about finding where we belong in the sermon? How do we listen for our own preaching voices and begin to incorporate them effectively? What exactly are we listening for? How do we go about detecting a preaching voice, let alone discerning its distinctiveness and developing its potential riches? How can we affirm this adventure in the face of worries that we will thereby lose our bearings and forget, in the midst of our self-listening, that it is God's word with which we are attempting to discover our particular way? We don't simply want to parrot God's word, but neither do we want to misrepresent it or drown it out in a wash of self-serving gestures and verbal flourishes.

The most obvious way to envision the place of a preaching voice in any sermon is to think in terms of proportion, balance, or even amount. "How much of *me* should I put in the sermon?" is how the question is often posed. While it may seem to serve our purposes readily, the quantitative approach is superficial and ultimately not very fruitful. How much is too much? Who can say? If the preacher's voice is regarded as something like a flavoring, condiment, or even as a significant ingredient in sermon fare, then "how much" becomes in large measure simply a matter of taste.

A more helpful approach, I think, is to place all these questions about our preaching voices in a much broader context. What might we discover about listening to our *own* voices by considering the ways in which we listen for *other* voices to which we need to pay attention when we preach? The sermon we deliver is not, in fact, a religious monologue; it is a sacred conversation. Perhaps our attempts to listen to ourselves will be illuminated by reflecting on how we listen to other partners in the sermon conversation.

Let's begin with the voices that have been recorded for us in the Scriptures. If the Scriptures are in some way a definitive witness to God's word, then they need to have their own say. They do not necessarily say what we want to hear or even what we can recognize without close attention. The Bible is not a catalog of ink blots with which we have license to free-associate.

Nor do the Scriptures speak with a single voice. There are layers upon layers of voices, all representing authors, editors, interpreters, poets, storytellers, chroniclers, and evangelists, some of whom are purposefully interacting with, even contending with, each other. The good news of God's love is revealed through a chorus of voices, many of which need to be patiently sorted out so that what registers in the hearer is not fragmented, distorted, or downright cacophonous.

Attentive, disciplined listening is essential for an understanding of the conversations taking place *in* Scripture. Such listening is also essential for establishing a clear and coherent conversation *with* Scripture. "What the Bible says" is important, but it won't do us any good if the only allowable response to that is dutiful silence.

"Don't talk back!" parents sometimes say to their children when they want to be obeyed. There may on occasion be some justification for such a clear conversation squelcher, but it is at best a risky gambit. Short of preventing the child from injury or danger, it not only threatens ongoing interaction and developing interpersonal relationships, it may also inhibit the very hearing it is meant to bring about.

It is riskier still to shut down conversation with the voices of Scripture. The ongoing dialogue of question and answer, statement and response is essential for understanding: "What does that text from Scripture really mean?" "How does this very ancient word apply to our current situation?" We can't even really hear

Scripture unless we "talk back" and so engage its many voices in extended and spirited conversation.

Who else, then, has a say in this sacred conversation that our sermons will attempt to convene? Individual voices in our congregations will contribute—teenager, single parent, corporate executive, member of a minority group who has been oh-so-deftly denied access to opportunities others take for granted. And in addition to the individual voices of those who gather on a Sunday, the congregation will also have a corporate voice.

Still other voices—some rather subtle, some quite strident—arise from many different dimensions of the culture in which we live: clashes of interest and irreconcilable values over national health care; virulent nationalisms that have risen to banish the hopes for peace and international community that welled up within us all at the end of the Cold War; entrenched bitterness in the community over a long-standing labor dispute. Such voices will either find their way coherently into the preaching conversation, or they will distract from the sermon in the way that the noise of passing traffic or a blaring siren invades the church sanctuary where people are listening to a sermon.

The patterns and practices of our worship also need to have their say, which include the routine rituals (formal or informal) that carry the community's expression of praise, confession, petition, and self-offering. These regular worship patterns are complemented by different prayers and portions of Scripture designated for particular days. The ordinary rhythms of a worshiping community are sharply punctuated by special days like Ash Wednesday, Easter, and Christmas, by individual life passage events like baptisms, weddings, and funerals, and by sudden urgent concerns and crises in the community. We never preach anywhere for very long at a stretch where we remain in a situation of "business as usual."

And alongside all these other voices there is also, inevitably, *your* voice, the voice of the preacher.

The task of a sermon is to elicit and to orchestrate all these voices into a word that is both clearly focused and richly resonant. Only when all of the voices are granted a hearing—both in their own right and in dialogue with each other—can preaching generate a stimulating sacred conversation in which the cleansing, comforting, and challenging word of God is discerned and carried into the witnessing conversations of the church as it goes forth from worship into the world. Since the Christian community gathers around the word of God that has come through history and been recorded in Scripture, biblical voices will be central to the preaching conversation. But they will not dominate it, nor demand that other voices not talk back.

Most of us have been taught that as preachers we need to exegete the texts of Scripture. We are also encouraged, as a matter of pastoral and practical necessity, to pay attention to the concerns of those in our congregations (so that our preaching will be "relevant"). If we have had comprehensive theological training, we will have been prepared to pay attention to our social surroundings and interpret the culture so that sermon listeners can envision the presence and the call of God in their personal and corporate situations. We may even have been encouraged to engage in careful liturgical planning, so that we can "make connections" between the sermon and the other elements in the worship service.

Concerning our own voices—the voice of the preacher—however, most of us have had much less help, if any. Chances are that help has boiled down to one of two proverbial injunctions: "Don't get in the way of the gospel" or "Be yourself." Perhaps you have even heard both maxims from the same mentors and practically in the same breath. It is difficult to fault either maxim as far as it goes, which is not far at all. Neither gives us much concrete guidance, and both seem more to contradict than to complement each other.

So how can we commence the process of listening to ourselves and of finding our proper place in the sacred sermon conversation? We can begin by observing that the purpose of listening to the voice that expresses our own distinctive experience is the same as the purpose of listening to all the other voices: so that, ultimately, in the dynamic interplay of many voices, the voice of God's Spirit can speak with freedom, power, and grace in the sermon.

With respect to our own voices, as with the others, there must be a preliminary listening. Not everything we hear will be included in what we actually preach. The recordings we take, as it were, are not simply spliced, one after another, onto a single super-tape labeled "Sermon." We would no more present an inventory of our personality or a catalog of our experiences in our preaching than we would quote at length from theological commentaries, deluge a congregation with demographic studies of urban conditions, tell personal stories revealed in sessions of pastoral counseling, or prattle on about liturgical rules and rubrics.

Still, we must do this preliminary listening with great care—not only to Scripture, congregation, culture, and liturgy, but also to ourselves. There is thus something of a parallel between listening to our own experience and to these other voices, or more accurately, communities of discourse.

There is a significant difference as well. Failure to pay attention to Scripture, culture, congregation, and liturgy will deny our sermon listeners access to significant information and, to some extent, subject them to our unexamined assumptions. Failure to pay attention to our own experience, on the other hand, will not prevent information about us from being revealed in our preaching. Unrecognized or unacknowledged by us, self-disclosure will tend to appear in our sermons and subtly but significantly interfere with our power to proclaim the gospel. Perhaps one of the reasons we feel odd about listening to our own sermon tapes is that we might have to face more of ourselves than we can manage to put up with at the moment!

"No one can successfully lie in the pulpit over an extended period of time," says O. C. Edwards. Similarly, I do not believe that any preacher will manage, either through intention or inattention, to prevent his or her preaching voice from significantly shaping the ways in which a congregation hears the word of God. One way or another, our congregations *will* hear "our way with God's word," so we might as well take an active hand in its responsible shaping.

Some of the listening—perhaps the most important listening that we do in the presence of all the various voices just discussed—is not sermon-specific. If the only time or way in which we pay attention to Scripture, culture, congregation, or liturgy is driven by the demands of an impending sermon, then our preaching will suffer severely over the long haul. It will take us more and more time to get fewer and fewer insights. Suffering the frustration of our apparent unproductivity, we may eventually curtail or abandon altogether what study time we do devote to specific sermon preparation. After all, it doesn't seem to be getting us anywhere. In all our disciplined listening, we must attend broadly, not just listen for something specific to say. It is not only irritating when someone enters a conversation bent on snatching information to serve a personal agenda; the information usually isn't worth much.

In listening specifically to our own experience, and to our preaching voice, what we will be looking for is not just a story or a personal reference with which to plug a gap in next Sunday's sermon. It will be a wide-ranging, open-ended effort to discern "what we sound like" rather than simply "what we have to say" about a subject. What we will be listening for as we attend to our own experience is not so much particular images, insights, and anecdotes that may be interesting or unusual, but the characteristic ways we have of engaging the world. We might then employ these ways in our preaching to articulate fresh approaches to God, new perspectives from which to see how God relates to us and imaginative ways of embodying the gospel's transforming power. If these can find their way into the sermon, the sermon will be not idolatrous self-disclosure, but incarnational engagement with the gospel.

The point of attending to your personal experience is to discern the particular ways in which God is present to you, and to celebrate those ways by using them, along with insights drawn from other voices, to frame and fill your preaching. Those among whom you preach will not have had the same experiences and perspectives as you do. If you are able clearly to understand and gracefully to appropriate your own experience, however, your listeners will be able to find points of contact—analogous experiences of their own through which they can recognize or discover God at work in their lives. Even though God's saving activity is universal, our discovery of that never comes through "generic" proclamation. In order to reach out *inclusively*, God always approaches us with *particulars*. The particulars with which you are most familiar are the particulars of your experience.

The sermon is a sacred conversation, and conversations are interactive. More must go on than everyone "putting in their two cents' worth," talking in sequence but talking past each other. A sermon is not a panel discussion or a morning talk show. Conversation is a much more intimate, integrated, interpersonal art. More than politeness is required ("Nice people don't interrupt when someone else has the floor"). Conversations can sometimes be leisurely, sometimes intense. There can be clashes in good conversations. Some conversations don't bring clear resolution or closure. In give-and-take conversations, what one person says will make a difference in what is said next, and by whom. Conversations both express and create community.

The preaching process joins a dialogue of questioning, explaining, celebrating, and responding to God's word in history, as that has been sampled in the Scriptures and borne in the developing life of the church in the world. A sermon extends that conversation into a very particular place at a very specific time. It will serve as a springboard for the ongoing process through which we, and those who come after us, experience God's power of health and healing. How absurd it is when preaching is treated simply as the "personal reflection" of the preacher! What a tragedy, on the other hand, when preachers do not bring all they are to the sacred conversation.

We can now begin to zero in more closely on how we go about discerning and developing our own distinctive preaching voices so that we can be fully effective conversation artists. The first and most important thing to be said sounds so obvious that we might be inclined to disregard it. Alan Jones states it succinctly: "The first law of the spiritual life is attention." Thomas Troeger echoes the principle in his fine little book, *Imagining a Sermon*: "Be attentive to what is."

This is not, however, as easy to understand, let alone to undertake, as it might seem. What we have to learn to do (and it takes a fair amount of practice) is to reflect upon various dimensions of our experience *descriptively* rather than *prescriptively*. We have to name whatever it is we find clearly, accurately, and completely rather than reporting it selectively, censoring it, or evaluating it as worthy or unworthy, as relevant or irrelevant to our preaching. *All* of our experience is fruitful material for reflection and for conscious appropriation, in one way or another, into our distinctive preaching voices. There is no indication whatsoever that Jesus called any of the first disciples for their special abilities, achievements, moral standing, or "promise for ministry." If anything, it just might have been for the splendidly diverse ways in which each of the apostles-in-the-making was a rogue!

"Be yourself!" is at best premature. The prime and prior question is, "What have I got here?" Most people who make a project of being themselves (in preaching, or elsewhere) haven't spent very much time doing their internal homework. They are all absorbed in trying to peddle what they don't even know they have!

Attention, then. Careful but not concentrated attention, not the kind of concentration that leaves wrinkles in your forehead. It is more a matter of making a regular practice of being alert to what catches you out of the corner of your eye. As with other dimensions of sermon listening, a specific methodology is helpful. That is, in fact, what much of the rest of this book lays out in detail and invites you to undertake.

For the moment, however, don't even worry about the "significance" of what you find, let alone "how it will preach." Just look and listen, smell and taste. Gently touch every dimension of your experience that you can get your hands on. You will find soft spots, hard callouses, tender places, rough textures, strong muscles, deep wounds, unexpected twists and turns. Every single one of these is a place from which you can learn, a place that has potential for spiritual insight, a place where God is present, often in surprising ways.

Notes

1. Phillips Brooks, *Lectures on Preaching* (Grand Rapids: Baker Book House, 1969; reprinted from the 1907 edition by E. P. Dutton Co., New York).

The Priest Who Lost His Voice

A Homiletical Meditation on the Calling of Zechariah

Luke 1:57-68

Once upon a time, there was a priest who lost his voice—
    right in the middle of the liturgy.

Chances are you've dreamed about that yourself
    at one time or another.

    The gospel is read.
    The congregation sits.
    Fits of coughing and fidgeting erupt,
      as folks settle in for the duration.
    Silence descends.
    You open your mouth to proclaim a polished, prophetic sermon.
    You open your mouth—
      and nothing comes out.

And then you wake up—
    breathing hard, drenched with sweat.

Dreams like that can send you scurrying to your psychoanalyst.
But there weren't any psychoanalysts for Zechariah to run to.
Besides, it wouldn't have done him any good.
He wasn't having a bad dream.

As Luke spins out this splendid piece of poetic theological drama,
    Zechariah is not being spooked by things that go bump in the night;
      he is being *blessed.*

Thrice-blessed, actually.
For openers, Zechariah gets a visit from the angel of the Lord,
    and he doesn't drop dead in his tracks.
That's no small favor, in itself.

Then Zechariah gets the promise of a gift—
    a gift beyond the bounds of his wildest, most wonderful dreams.

And finally he gets to give up his voice for a while.
With all the sermons you and I are supposed to preach,
    we should be so lucky!

It isn't always a good thing to lose your preaching voice.
    If you lose it because, like a gangly, pimpley-faced adolescent boy,
        your voice is changing out from under you,
            and you just can't keep it from cracking
                at the most embarrassing moments—
    well, that can be downright painful.

    If you lose your preaching voice because you have lost your nerve,
        that is a deep tragedy.

    If you lose your voice because you have lost your heart,
        that is a very great anguish indeed.

    If you lose your preaching voice because other people have ignored it,
        ridiculed it, or shouted it down,
            over and over, time after time—
    if you lose your voice because it is forever getting squelched—
        that is an outrage.

    If you lose your preaching voice because, one morning,
        you wake up and find that you no longer *dare* to speak of the God
            in whose name you have, for too long, *failed* to speak—
            that is not a good way to lose your voice.

But Zechariah did not lose his voice in any of those ways.

A once-over-lightly reading of Luke chapter one can give you the impression
    that Zechariah is being punished for his incredulity:
        "How will I know?" he asks the angel, skeptically.
        "I'm too old to have a child—and so is my wife!"

But really now, granted the circumstances, what else is he supposed to say:
    "Why yes, of course, and thank you very much"?

If, for years, you had been old enough to be a grandpa,
    how would *you* react, if you were told
        that you were about to be a brand-new dad?

Mary, after all, asks a very similar question of Gabriel
    on the second stop of the angel's natal announcement run:
        "How can this be?"

Like Zechariah, Mary challenges Gabriel—reasonably enough.
And Mary doesn't get zapped.
She gets a sign—a token in pledge of the gift to come.
And so, I suspect, does Zechariah.

Have you ever been blessed with a good long bout of laryngitis?
At first you struggle to shove some sound
    through vocal cords that have gone on strike.
Then you resort to wide gestures, vigorous scribbles,
    and exaggerated facial expressions.
Sooner or later, you just settle down and shut up.

And then you start to hear things you don't often get a chance to hear.
    Other people, for openers.
    You hear them, not just more, or better,
        but differently, more deeply.
    You start listening to the self
        your very own speech sometimes all but suffocates.
    You listen to sounds in the world.
    You listen to the silence.

And when you find your voice again—for a little while, at least—
    you are tuned in to whole new levels of resonance and dissonance
        in all the voices that are parties to your conversations.

I imagine it being something like that when Zechariah loses his voice.
It's a blessing that is both a promise,
    and a preparation for a greater blessing.

So, what are we about in this book of homiletical reflection?
Not an artificially induced experience of homiletical laryngitis,
    but an invitation, nonetheless, to the kind of deeper listening
        that quiet, careful, inner conversation brings.

Let's face it.
We preachers tend to talk too much.

Let me speak for myself:
I am constantly tempted, instinctively disposed,
    to talk without listening long enough, widely enough, deeply enough.

And that is a great danger,
    because the single most important task
        that you and I have as preachers of the gospel
        is to become good listeners—
            listeners to conversations that still resound in ancient texts;
            listeners to shrill cries and subtle background murmurs in our culture;
            listeners to the shared concerns and individual insights
                of those who make up our constantly changing congregations.
        Listeners as well to our own voices,
            and to the voices of others who preach in partnership with us.

The object in this book is not to induce homiletical laryngitis.
It is, however, to shape some space for quiet contemplation
    about what it means for each of us to preach.

But that is not at all the same thing as homiletical narcissism,
    or even homiletical therapy.

We need to attend with great care to our own distinctive preaching voices—
    but for the same reason that we need to listen to voices
      in Scripture, in culture, and in our congregations.
We need to listen to these voices, so that, in and through them all,
    we can more clearly discern an unspeakably wilder Word,
      a Word that shatters all human words, even as it sustains them.

From Zechariah and Elizabeth, members of the priestly establishment,
    there comes forth a prophet named John,
      whose own clear word falls like a sharp axe
        on rotten religious wood.

But Zechariah is far more than a passive progenitor
    in this process of prophetic birthing.
Gracefully silenced, so that he can more carefully attend,
    Zechariah the old priest is given back his voice.
Given not simply a voice transplant—
    given, rather, a richer, more resounding version of his *own true* voice.

Reconnected with the voices of his own preaching parents,
    God's holy prophets of old,
      Zechariah bursts forth in the song of a mighty savior,
        a savior who will free the oppressed for a new kind of service—
          service in holiness and righteousness,
          service without fear.

Zechariah's prophetic songburst is revolutionary politics
    fueled and focused in a celebration of praise.
Blessed *by* God, Zechariah proclaims:
    "Blessed *be* God—
      A God who comes to visit chosen people,
        to visit them and set them free."

Zechariah can sing that truth from the top of his lungs,
    because it is a truth he has experienced first-hand.

As our social fabric disintegrates,
    outstripping our capacity to patch it up,

many preachers feel an understandable concern,
an almost frantic urgency, to preach a "prophetic" word.

But this is a time for listening,
as much as a time for speaking.
Indeed, the more pressing the need for prophetic speaking,
the more critical the need for patient, probing listening—
to Scripture, culture, congregation,
to ourselves, and to each other's preaching.

God burst in on faithful old Zechariah
as he was crooning along the best he could.
God blessed Zechariah,
not only with a son who had a good, strong voice,
but also with a fresh way of using his own voice—
a voice, I wager, that Zechariah hardly knew he had.

With all the sermons God is calling us to preach,
with all the variations on the song of deliverance
God is calling us to sing;
I cannot think that we will be less graced,
as we listen with expectation for the distinctive sound
of our own preaching voices.

■ Part II ■

Discerning Your Particular Preaching Gifts

■ 3 ■

Homiletical Resources Ready-to-Hand

Naming the Treasures in Your Own Field

We have talked thus far about beginning a sermon conversation among the voices of Scripture, culture, congregation, liturgy, and preacher. We have also acknowledged that Scripture, culture, congregation, and liturgy do not speak with a single voice. All of these are "communities of discourse," rich centers of conversations in themselves. Is the preacher an exception to this?

At first it might seem so. Few pulpits are large enough to accommodate more than a single occupant, and (mercifully) the "dialogue sermon" seems to have run its course as a passing homiletical fad. Yet a bit of reflection makes it obvious that each "individual" preacher also contains within him or herself a rich community of discourse; each preacher is a conversation center as well. The title of a book by Elizabeth O'Connor says it nicely: *Our Many Selves.*

None of us initially learned how to talk in a vacuum. We were all born into conversational networks, and our understanding of language started to develop well before we were able to participate as players in the game. There is no way we can radically segregate our own words from the words of the communities that have given us the gift of speech.

Students of philosophy often say that the Enlightenment was spawned from the troubled musings of a French Jesuit named Descartes, who was deeply concerned to avoid falling into any of the errors that might be lurking around in the language of his culture. So he resolved to sequester himself and systematically disregard any truth claims that did not come with unimpeachable credentials. In the isolation of a stove-heated room, he quickly found himself reduced to knowing nothing for certain except the existence of his own agonizing questions. Fortunately (in his own mind at least) he came upon some keys to unlock the doors of his self-imposed solitary confinement cell. Philosophers ever since have disputed whether or not he really did manage to unlock the door, or whether he surreptitiously slid out a convenient window instead.

Was Descartes really able to leave his community and his culture outside when he entered his room and shut the door? Hardly. His community was in there with him, unacknowledged but still embedded in the very thought processes of his skepticism. It is tempting to say that the beginnings of the Enlightenment were not very enlightened, for no matter how unique or original our ways of speaking may seem to be, they are inextricably rooted in the context of linguistic relationships.

Any talk of our distinctive preaching voices, therefore, must honor these ongoing connections—with language, culture, and personal relationships, and also with our faith communities. As preachers, says Harry Pritchett, we always enter the pulpit in procession. So the search for our distinctive preaching voices will be anything but an exercise in homiletical narcissism. Instead, it will be a careful attempt to listen to patterns of community interaction and response, with an ear alert to our particular learnings from and contributions to these various conversations. Whatever else we are as preachers, we are members of one body who cannot say to one another "I have no need of you."

On the other hand, just because there is nothing in our preaching that we can strictly call our own, it does not follow that we are clones of our culture or our church. Our preaching is never simply a passing on of previous material, unmarked by our personal shaping.

Some religious traditions like to claim otherwise. If preachers are merely channels of God's word, then listeners don't have to worry about their errors, slants, biases, or axe-grindings, intentional or unconscious. Such a perspective on preaching might be nice, but it doesn't happen. It is itself a decisive slant. And, if Phillips Brooks is right, preaching that succeeds in being "free" of the preacher's personhood would not itself be true to the gospel it was trying to proclaim.

I suspect that most of us do not identify with such a perspective. We do not regard the preacher as simply a fax machine charged with transmitting memos from the Almighty. But many of us are vulnerable to another, more subtle, perhaps more dangerous form of authoritarianism. We can see it at work in those of us who attend continuing education courses in preaching and fill our shelves with books by the latest preaching superstar. Eager to give our preaching a shot in the arm, we explain on arrival, "I have come to this preaching conference because I just want to sit at the feet of [fill in the blank with the authority of choice]!" We bring what we regard as our empty cups and ask the experts to fill them up.

Preaching experts *do* have their place. That place, however, is not to tell us what to say or how to say it, but rather to engage us in reflective conversation so that, in the matrix of shared speech, we can each discover afresh what God would have us say, and how we are distinctively graced to say it. All of us need regular renewal, and preaching luminaries have a role in that. But before assuming that something in us is inadequate or has gone awry, and that we therefore need to avail ourselves of an outside expert, we might attend to what is there in us already—what we may have never noticed, have long forgotten, or never thought much about. What we will discover, as we listen to our many selves, are deep wellsprings of creativity and sources of homiletical spirituality.

There is no single way of focusing our attention on what those dimensions are. In this book I suggest a pattern that may be helpful in your process of discernment. We will spend time visiting a number of different persons, places, and things and will be asking ourselves several questions with respect to our preaching:

- Who got me going?
- What have I been about?
- How do I tend to operate?
- When do I resonate most clearly?
- With what may my preaching be compared?
- Where do I feel connected?
- Why do I bother?

When heading into new territory, I often need both a map and accompanying directions. Such a map is provided at the end of this chapter. It shows at a glance how the chapters in Part II are related as stages of an unfolding adventure in homiletical self-discovery. The points on the map (with their corresponding chapters) represent, I believe, important landmarks in the "soul geography" of any preacher.

Here are some suggestions for making good use of the map and for pacing yourself along the journey into which this book invites you.

■ First, don't mistake the map for the journey. Bird's-eye views can be misleading. With normal road maps, there is not the slightest tendency to think that you have actually gone from Buffalo to Baltimore if you have simply traced with your finger the line on the map that represents the road between the city in New York and the city in Maryland. With conceptual road maps, however, it is possible to convince yourself that, just because you have seen a cluster of connected concepts, you have therefore actually made the trip. However revealing in its own right, a bird's-eye view is not the same as the feel of the ground under your feet.

■ Second, it can be a valuable experience to undertake this journey as an individual preacher. (Indeed, there is no other way to take much of it.) Nevertheless, your journey will be significantly enriched if you take it along with a small group of colleagues. Your preaching voice is not meant to be heard echoing from a solitary canyon, declaimed as a soliloquy, or spoken into a tape recorder in the privacy of your own room. Sermon tapes made in a studio instead of in a live worship setting always sound like the canned productions that they are. In the process of trying to learn about your own distinctive voice as a preacher, you will best hear how you sound by entering a conversation with some of your colleagues about each other's preaching. There are certain advantages in any collegial enterprise, but the need to hear your own preaching voice in conversation with others is, I think, integral to the success of this particular venture. After all, preaching is an ongoing conversation.

■ Third, as you have probably already seen by thumbing through the book, white space is provided throughout so that you can record your reflections right here rather than having to read the questions and then go off to think about them, or find someplace else to write them down. You may want to use the space to record impressions raw, just as they come to you. Or you may prefer to photocopy some of the question pages, cut them up, and paste them in a journal where you will have more space. You may be more comfortable writing on a computer or word processor. You may wish to record initial reflections elsewhere, and later summarize your insights here.

■ Fourth, complete sentences are fine as responses to questions posed in each section, but don't restrict yourselves to these. Sentence fragments, free-floating phrases, stray words, pictures, diagrams, and doodles—write in whatever style is comfortable for you.

■ Fifth, don't be compulsive about digging out data in detail for every question that is posed. Some questions will stimulate more awareness than others. Some questions may suggest not answers, but other questions of your own—questions more directly relevant to your own experience. Follow where they lead you. Questions that don't spark much insight now may direct you toward more fruitful ground at some future date.

■ Sixth, whatever else you do, don't try to barrel on through the whole journey in a single sitting. If you do, either you will hear practically nothing at all, or you will hear so much that you hear nothing clearly (like being in a noisy, crowded room). The excursion of this book is meant to be a source of recreation, a vacation. It would be a real shame if you turned it into work—a job to be completed as quickly as you can!

■ Finally, some sections may strike you as more fruitful than other sections. Within each section, some questions will engage you more than others. Linger over what invites you to stop and chat awhile. Pass lightly over questions that don't seem to call your name. Wander about in the questions during your free time: try not to undertake them as a protracted essay examination you must rush to complete before the ringing of the bell.

Some suggestions for your focusing will be offered here and there as to why particular questions are posed, or how your responses might be relevant for your preaching ministry. For the time being, however, just attend and describe. In addition to the suggestions that are offered along the way, the chapters in Part III attempt to cluster your observations and insights around the bottom-line question of "How can this preach?"

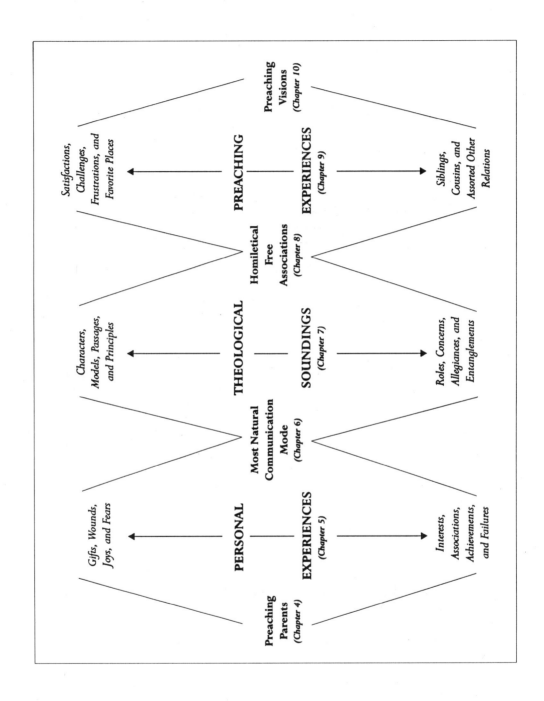

Who Got Me Going?

Ghosts and Graces From Our Preaching Parents

"**Y**ou certainly are a chip off the old block!" Not so many years ago, that was a way of making small talk out of a truism: children are in many ways affected by their parents. "The sins of the parents are visited upon the children." A great many years ago, that was a way of making an important point: regardless of how free we human beings think we are, nobody comes with a clean slate. Family ghosts have a way of coming back to haunt us.

That is hardly news in the age after Freud. But while we acknowledge the pervasive influence of our biological and sociological heritage, we seldom stop to think of how the principle applies with respect to our homiletical heritage. Anyone who has gone to church with any regularity has pulpit ancestors—preachers who have modeled, for good or ill, what a sermon is supposed to sound like: how long, how loud, how laced with Scripture references, how esoteric, or how heart-rending it should be. Whenever you stand up to begin a sermon, there is a cloud of unseen witnesses behind you. They will not step forth to introduce themselves, but they are present. And they are not silent.

Having pulpit ancestors is not necessarily a bad thing. Competent preachers constantly employ the voices of their "preaching parents" effectively with their own distinctive preaching gifts. But this is more likely to happen when the voices of our preaching parents are identified and clearly distinguished from our own—regardless of whether the preachers we have grown up with have been "good" or "bad." Good and bad models can have both good and bad effects. Poor preaching parents may have so irritated your ears when you were a captive listener that, ever since the day you started preaching, you have never been tempted to repeat their homiletical mistakes. Yet children often grow up to ape the actions of parents unintentionally, and in our preaching, we may find ourselves doing some of the things we swore we would never do.

You were blessed indeed if you grew up with good preaching—blessed to a point that can become a bane. "If only I could preach like Father Scroggins!" you lament, sometimes only half-consciously. The difficulty, of course, is that Father Scroggins, like every other human being, is one of a kind. What an exercise in frustration if you try to emulate the qualities of a preacher you have idealized but have no capacity for reproducing! Unless you are able to leave the nest and cut the apron strings, you will end up doing halfway decent Scroggins imitations but never discover the distinctive configuration of gifts that can only be orchestrated through your own voice.

Shaping a preaching voice can be particularly challenging for women in the pulpit whose preaching parents have only been male. If what it means to preach has been transmitted without appropriate translation from one gender, ethnic, racial, or cultural context to another, learning to preach authentically can be very hard. I think of a number of Chinese preaching students I have taught who, for some time, insisted on sounding like British colonials instead of like themselves. We need to celebrate the gifts and learn from the mistakes of our preaching parents, to identify fruitful points of contact with them and clearly define our differences.

What do you remember about your preaching parents, about the sermons they preached that moved you to joy, commitment, terror, or disgust? How did those sermons work? What themes, styles, or patterns of illustration permeated them or recurred in them? In what ways do your sermons imitate those sermons? How do they express your homiletical rebellion? The following questions in this chapter are intended to help you bring to light the ghosts and graces you have been given from your preaching parents.

1 What was the best sermon you remember hearing? What was the worst?

2 What can you remember in general about sermons you have heard?

3 Who were the most influential preachers to whom you have listened?

4 What was distinctive about what they said, or how they preached?

5 What in their personalities created a lasting impression in you?

6 What particular style, flavor, focus, or pattern did their sermons have?

7 What have your experiences of sermons and preachers taught you about what makes for good or bad preaching?

8 How does your own preaching conform to those ideals? Where is there a lack of congruence? Does this lack of congruence represent a conscious shift on your part? Or a deliberate act of healthy homiletical defiance?

9 At what points are your preaching parents pinching and constricting the way you preach? What are the ghosts? What are the graces?

10 Where would you like your preaching to move in relation to the ghosts and graces? Can you track ways in which you have already taken these positive and negative influences in your own directions?

It may be helpful here to reflect upon the way in which the covenant communities described in Scripture are woven as a fabric of ancestral relations. Think of Elijah and Elisha, of Paul and Timothy, of Naomi and Ruth.

It is quite likely that additional insights will emerge later on as you put this cluster of questions on the back burner. Recognizing that we will revisit this territory again, we turn now to some points of personal orientation.

■ 5 ■

What Have I Been About?

Personal Experiences That Create a Context

Two assumptions tend to drive our current cultural understanding of the relation between life and work: 1) what happens to us outside of our job is on our own time; and 2) when we change jobs, we can't depend on getting credit for previous experience. In the normal run of the work-a-day world, there is often no connection between who we are and what we do. This system has certain advantages: if we do our jobs well, what goes on in the rest of our lives is nobody's business (unless, of course, you are a politician). Our privacy is preserved, and considerations irrelevant to our competence and performance are kept out of court.

Similarly, what we know about other types of employment does not automatically earn us any special favors when we change jobs. The burden of proof is clearly on us to show the relevance of our former work experience to the positions for which we are applying. That way there is, supposedly, a level playing field for all applicants. We work our way up the ladder based on our expertise and our seniority. That makes competition cleaner than it would be if we were forever having to deal with everybody's previous lives.

Most people bring these assumptions about work and life to the preaching vocation, with some validity. What you have learned as a cosmetologist, bricklayer, or attorney will not help you much with biblical exegesis. Just because you feel a call to preach, it does not follow that you are equipped or should be licensed to do so, based solely on your sense of call and your life experience. But while it is true that distinctive professional training is important for those who preach, it is not true that previous life and work experiences have no significant bearing on your preaching.

Personal histories and previous work experience are not out-of-bounds in the preaching domain. The metaphor of domain or turf does not fit in this case. The many dimensions of one's experience in the preaching life do not have to compete or even overlap; they can blend like instruments in an orchestra, or interweave like threads in a tapestry.

Dimensions of a preaching life imply and rely upon one another, operating in and through one another. Certain pieces drawn from your previous experience can sometimes illuminate theological truths, and can be employed effectively as sermon illustrations. I remember a skilled plastic surgeon who, in mid-life, was preparing for a second career as a priest. He had a rich reservoir of medical stories from which to draw, and a fairly good sense of how and where these stories fit. This, to him, was the appropriate way of using his prior experience.

A deeper understanding of this connection, however, came from an athletic young woman who had been actively involved in the arts and in recreation. "Oh! I see!" she suddenly burst out in the midst of a discussion of the tasks and methods of preaching. "A preacher is like a square dance caller!" An unexpected, but very fruitful connection.

Indeed, the less obvious the point of contact between your former life and your preaching life, the more likely it is that a profoundly illuminating connection may be sparked. Imagination can build powerful bridges between apparently far-flung territories. "As a professional city map-maker, what special insights do you bring to the preaching task?" I once asked an entering seminarian. "I don't see any," was the immediate reply.

Do you? More to the point, what do you see when you look at *your* personal experience? Look first at things that have happened to you, then, in the following section, at things you have done.

Gifts, Wounds, Joys, and Fears:
conditions that give our voices color

Much of what we deal with in life are the "givens." Sometimes these givens seem very much like gifts; at other times we would like to write "refused" and send them back where they came from. The next set of questions invites you to explore the conditions that have shaped your life. The focus here is on what has *happened* to you, since your life experiences will inevitably color your preaching. This is not to say that your preaching is forever conditioned by the conditions under which you operate. Your experiences set a context within which you can make responsible determinations as to how your preaching voice will enter into dialogue with the other voices that make up the sermon conversation.

1 What have been your most significant positive and negative personal relationships

■ with family members?

■ with friends?

■ with business associates?

■ with competitors of various sorts?

2 What are some of your deepest

- joys?

- griefs?

- angers?

- fears?

- shames?

- longings?

■ hopes?

■ dreams?

■ impish impulses?

---

3 What kind of architectural spaces do you most and least enjoy?

---

4 What kind of outdoor places do you enjoy most? Are you a country person or a city person?

---

5 How has your experience been markedly affected by

■ your gender?

■ your race?

■ your educational background?

■ your economic situation?

■ your sexual orientation?

6 What kinds of experiences bring out your strongest emotional energy—positive or negative?

7° As a child, what did you want to be when you grew up (besides a preacher)? What vocational fantasies do you still entertain?

8 What are your most idiosyncratic characteristics? (If people knew you thought, felt, or acted that way, they would think you were really weird!)

9 Describe some of your prominent tastes in literature, drama, art, and music.

10 Are you a "spring" person? Or is your personality more akin to summer, fall, or winter?

11 Are you more of an extrovert or an introvert? How does this predisposition manifest itself in the way you operate with yourself and with others? (Do you talk with others in order to figure out what you have to say, or do you wait to speak until your ideas are fully formulated?)

12 What sort of vocational and avocational skills (or lack thereof) were you brought up with? What did your parents, grandparents, other relations and family acquaintances do in their jobs and in their free time?

13 What patterns of personal and corporate prayer do you find most conducive to your spiritual well-being?

14 What would you really like to be able to do before you die?

What you have encountered here is, of course, a kaleidoscope. There may or may not be any clear or fixed patterns apparent to you right now. The particular relevance of any experience may emerge only as a spark, an "aha," as you find yourself in conversation with the Scriptures, with issues of the day, with concerns of those among whom you preach. New pieces of significant experience may emerge in your memory as you actively engage these other voices. So don't shut down this process with a summary. Consider, rather, Jacob at Jabbok Brook. The angel wrestles with him, wounds him, names him, and blesses him. How might significant experiences you have undergone be seen as such angelic visitations?

Interests, Associations, Achievements, and Failures: activities that give our voices range

You respond to life as well as react to it. What are some of your "doings"? How have they gone successfully? How have they failed miserably? How do they hang in the balance? What is the significance of these for what you understand yourself to be at your center? Reflect a bit on how far and in what different directions your activities have taken you. How wide ranging are your experiences? With what distinctive slices of life are you on speaking terms? In the questions that follow, concentrate on the areas that seem most pertinent—for whatever reason, or for no reason.

---

1 What jobs have you held? What careers have you undertaken other than the ordained ministry?

2 What did you find fulfilling and frustrating in those careers or jobs?

3 What hobbies or interests have you pursued or always wanted to pursue?

4 What role do you take in

- sports?

- the performing arts?

- community service activities?

5 What was the greatest disaster you have experienced in enterprises you have undertaken?

6 What interests have you abandoned voluntarily? Under pressure?

7 What would you characterize as your most significant learning experiences?

8 How do you keep up with what is going on in the world—especially in areas beyond your immediate environment? What kind of reading do you do? What in that reading do you most enjoy?

9 What traveling have you done? What interaction in cross-cultural contexts? What languages do you know beyond your native tongue? What languages have you always wanted to learn? Why?

10 What do you regard as your "cutting edges"—areas of curiosity and insatiable appetite for learning?

11 What familiar persons, places, and things do you return to visit for refreshment and renewal, solace and strength?

12 The previous categories are far from exhaustive: carve out some spaces of your own, and see how they fill in. What else do you need to say about what you have done in your life?

Experiences are potential windows on the gospel and on the preaching task, but they also can keep the light out. How can a single experience at once illuminate and obscure? Take some of your responses in this section and revisit them with this question in mind. For example, how might a career in the military, in medicine, or in metallurgy tend to restrict your vision of who God is and how God works? What would be the result if, in your preaching, people only heard about God's mighty acts in terms of conquest and order, diagnosis and prescription, or smelting and forging?

For the present, it is more important to leave things a little blurred around the edges than to stack your experiences neatly on a set of shelves. Still, you might ask yourself, "What new connections among these experiences do I see? In what directions does my life seem to be moving?" As you reflect upon the projects of your life, you might remember the Apostle Paul, who was able in his correspondence with young churches to list his failures without crippling guilt, and to assert his splendid achievements without false humility. Grace produced for Paul a wide-angle lens through which he was able to perceive and interpret the gospel. How wide is the range of your homiletical vision?

How Do I Tend to Operate?

Communication Patterns That Give Our Voices Shape

In this chapter there is only one question: Do you identify yourself primarily as a poet, a storyteller, or an essay-writer? No preacher is exclusively a poet, storyteller, or essayist, of course; effective preachers regularly use elements of each in all of their sermons. But most preachers have a voice which is centered more in one mode of discourse than another.

If a preacher operates incessantly from one mode, listeners will begin to typecast the sermons and lose interest. Eminently predictable sermons seldom catch folks up in the surprising dimensions of grace. Different circumstances call for different strategies and different sermon shapes. It remains true, however, that most of us function more naturally in one mode than another. We can do a more effective job of reaching beyond our respective comfort zones if we are first able to identify and happily inhabit them. So, poet, storyteller, or essay-writer—from which center do you listen and speak most comfortably in everyday speech, and in sermons?

How would you know? You might begin by asking yourself the sorts of questions that have come to be regarded as standard in any personality inventory, such as the Myers-Briggs or the Enneagram. You might ask yourself about the ways in which you most effectively receive, process, retain, and communicate information. All of that has a bearing. There has been some work done on how people with different personality types tend to preach and hear sermons, and what happens when preachers and congregations are type-crossed—as they often are.

It is possible that you may have reflected on some of this material in response to certain questions in the previous sections. The focus here, however, is a bit more directly related to your task in preaching as a communication artist (or, more precisely, a conversation artist). The questions that get to the heart of the matter ask, How do you do things with words? How do you receive them? How do you reckon with them? Reveal with them? How do you reconcile, or rejuvenate with them?

■ Do you experience and express words primarily in terms of their sensuous or evocative potential—the way a poet hears and offers language?

■ Do you experience and express words primarily in terms of how they convey action, interaction, drama, narrative—the energy center of a storyteller?

■ Do you experience and express words primarily in terms of their ability to summarize, analyze, and criticize concepts—the reflective, abstractive capacity of language that is engaged by the essayist, the jurist, the philosopher?

Words, as such, are not poems, stories, or essays. Very few individual phrases or single sentences are, either. Paragraphs, however—now we are moving away from poetry in the direction of an essay. Paragraphs often appear in stories, of course, but they tend to function differently there than they do in expository prose. And if there is no action language in the story—no direct or indirect dialogue, no movement of anything other than thought—then we are talking philosophical novel at best.

By now you will realize that my words at this point are functioning in the "essay" category. My language here is primarily conceptual, whereas in preceding material I have also used language more imagistically and evocatively. Later in this chapter, in one of the sermons on one of Jesus' parables in Matthew 13, I am preaching a sermon by telling a story.

What kind of a natural speaker and listener are you? What is your most natural pattern of communication? If you aren't clear about that, perhaps you can tease it out by asking yourself the following questions.

1 Does your attention spontaneously perk up or start to lag when language is being used primarily to:

a) prove a point?
b) create a visual scene or evoke a sensory awareness?
c) produce a music-like effect?
d) describe a tense situation?
e) explain a position?
f) connect one image with another?
g) bring everyone up-to-date on what happened?
h) set matters in context?
i) evoke or express an emotion?
j) celebrate a special event?
k) remove an objection?
l) define an important idea?
m) tell a joke (not a riddle)?
n) explain how a certain situation came to be?
o) take the listener on a journey?

Options a, e, h, k, and l tend to be indicative of language used in its essay mode. Poetic uses are closely connected with b, c, f, i, and j. The functions fulfilled in alternatives d, g, m, n, and o are more aligned with storytelling. Which options do you employ most frequently in your own speaking?

2 As you review some of the more significant sermons that you remembered in chapter 4, are the mental hooks that hold them in memory for you a theological position well argued? a vivid lingering sensory or emotional impression? the plot of a story from Scripture, church history, or some situation in contemporary life?

3 When you are in conflict yourself or you are attempting to assist someone in conflict, do you tend to reach for good reasons, a similar situation that others had to work through, or a fresh way of seeing the problem?

4 If you were to describe the essence of the gospel in a nutshell, would your witness sound more like a parable, a psalm, or a creed?

5 If you are describing a sermon that you have heard (or one of your own), would you most likely resort to a picture sketched, a propositional statement, or a dramatic scene?

6 Do you find it most engaging to deliver a sermon from a biblical narrative, a Pauline epistle, a psalm or proverb, a prophetic image (Amos' plumb line, Ezekiel's valley), or an image from the Sermon on the Mount? (It might be interesting to review your sermons from the last six months to see which types tend to pop up most frequently.)

Comparing Your Way with Others

Another way to hone in on your most natural sermon-shaping style is for you to compare your style with the styles of other preachers. Listen now to three sermons, each of which is configured primarily in one of the three patterns we have identified: poet, essayist, and storyteller. You may get a clearer sense of how you most frequently preach by comparing your own way with words with the ways these preaching colleagues are using words.

In order to illustrate more clearly the distinctive preaching patterns, the text of these three sermons is the same: the Parable of the Wheat and the Tares found in Matthew 13. These sermons are not ideal types in the sense of being examples of perfect sermons (those don't exist, remember?), nor are they put forward so that you can rank or grade them against each other. Listen so that you can observe their different rhetorical shapes. You will note immediately that elements of poetic, narrative, and expository styles appear in each sermon, just as in everyday speech the interweaving of such rhetorical elements is continuous. Still, with little difficulty you will probably hear that the weight or thrust is clearly different from one sermon to another.

One sermon was delivered by an experienced parish priest, another by a seminary student, and the third arises out of my experience as a teacher of preaching. The other preachers are women from two different denominational traditions. Listen with an ear to what these sermons do with you, and how they make that happen. Ask not just what each sermon is saying, but how each sermon is working and to which you respond most readily.

The Parable of the Wheat and the Tares
Matthew 13:24-30, 36-43

Jesus put before them another parable: "The kingdom of heaven may be compared to someone who sowed good seed in his field; but while everybody was asleep, an enemy came and sowed weeds among the wheat, and then went away. So when the plants came up and bore grain, then the weeds appeared as well. And the slaves of the householder came and said to him, 'Master, did you not sow good seed in your field? Where, then, did these weeds come from?' He answered, 'An enemy has done this.' The slaves said to him, 'Then do you want us to go and gather them?' But he replied, 'No; for in gathering the weeds you would uproot the wheat along with them. Let both of them grow together until the harvest; and at harvest time I will tell the reapers, Collect the weeds first and bind them in bundles to be burned, but gather the wheat into my barn.'"

....

Then he left the crowds and went into the house. And his disciples approached him, saying, "Explain to us the parable of the weeds of the field." He answered, "The one who sows the good seed is the Son of Man; the field is the world, and the good seed are the children of the kingdom; the weeds are the children of the evil one, and the enemy who sowed them is the devil; the harvest is the end of the age, and the reapers are angels. Just as the weeds are collected and burned up with fire, so will it be at the end of the age. The Son of Man will send his angels, and they will collect out of his kingdom all causes of sin and all evildoers, and they will throw them into the furnace of fire, where there will be weeping and gnashing of teeth. Then the righteous will shine like the sun in the kingdom of their Father. Let anyone with ears listen!"

A. The Preacher as Poet:
a sermon shaped by images

It's not a very good time to be a weed. The open-air markets are teeming with all sorts of produce: luscious tomatoes, ripe melons, fresh corn-on-the-cob, watermelon. People are "oohing" and "ahing" as they sort through the abundance of farmers' toils. Wheat, beans, corn: feed crops are just starting to be harvested and sent to market. It's been a very good year—lots of rain (but not too much) and sunshine—we can all rejoice that this year will mean money in the pockets of our farmers, and delightful repasts of freshness at our tables for weeks to come.

Unless you are a weed. Weeds do not find their way to the market to be chosen for a special picnic, or in the big trucks on their way to the feed auction. Instead, they lie on fallow ground, rotting in the hot August sun. In the days before technology, they met an even more terrible fate: they were burned as fuel in fires which dried the grain by whose side they had grown for months.

No, it's not a good time to be a weed. Time was, however, that being a weed wasn't much different from being the wheat. Sown alongside the wheat, weeds had the benefit of the sun and rain. Fertilizer is not discriminating—into the roots of wheat and weeds alike, it nourished each. Root structures, stems and leaves of both wheat and weed thrived. Pesticides limited the damage done by worms and bugs—protecting, again, both wheat and weed. In those days, you could be wheat or weed, and life was pretty much the same.

Well, some of us farmers would have uprooted those darn weeds right from the start. In my zealous gardening, I have faced weeds with a vengeance only to discover that, early on, those tender little shoots which I though were pesky weeds were the beginning of carrots, or onions, or corn. I learned, the hard way, that sometimes it is far better to let those weeds grow up right beside your prized cabbage, than to risk uprooting the cabbage along with the weeds.

There is a moral here somewhere, I suspect. Just as in the parable of the weeds in the wheat, Jesus is telling us something. At first, it seems to be a story about all the misfits in a community whom we "allow" to exist alongside all the faithful. Someday, if we are just patient enough, we will be relieved of their presence. The word seems to be that, were we to uproot those "weeds" from our midst too early, perhaps some of us "good" Christians might be hurt in the process. So let's just be patient. They'll get theirs in the end.

But I think that's only partially right. (And it's the "partially" that's dangerous.) Yes, the weeds will be separated from the wheat in the end. Yes, Jesus is saying that uprooting weeds before the harvest can do damage to the tender shoots of wheat. But what a self-righteous attitude ("I, of all, am wheat!") ignores is just *who* is doing the harvesting,...*who* is commanding the reaping and burning. The householder is God himself. Lest our smugness, and judgment of others deceive us, let us remember it is not the wheat who harvests itself. And just as the weeds are hidden among the wheat, so are our sins hidden, at times, from us.

Does this mean everyone has to endure a paranoid existence until the end harvest? That we don't know whether we are weed or wheat? I don't think so. I think what it means is that we look to the householder to glean the good from the bad in his final harvest—including the transformation of our own souls. We will be at once saved and cleansed, made new, fully wheat. That which is in us, and others, which is essentially weed will be burned.

The temptation is to take this task on ourselves. To root out evil things in our midst—eradicate those whose values, life-styles, or ethics do not exactly correlate with what we think it means to be wheat. But in many cases we are not eliminating weeds so much as uprooting tender shoots which are really wheat among us. And we are much better at calling others weeds than we are at looking at ourselves and how we choke the life from the wheat.

Jesus tells us in his story to wait, just as the farmers have waited all these months for the abundance which we have before us. This doesn't mean that we don't tend our Christian community as proper stewards should. We should fertilize and protect it, upbuild and support it. But the harvest is the householder's. The separation of the wheat from the weeds belongs to God. Praise be to God, who makes us wheat in the end!

B. The Preacher as Essayist:
a sermon shaped by arguments

It has been a few years since *Time* magazine ran a series of articles surveying the contemporary religious consciousness of Americans. Do you remember the one saying that the vast majority of our citizenry believed in hell, but that only a tiny fraction of them thought there was any likelihood that they were going there? Most, however, could name someone who was.

At this point, I do not remember if there were some common denominators among the favored candidates for the dubious honors of hellfire and damnation. But it would be an interesting exercise; for by studying what a society rejects, you learn a lot about what a society is. The particulars of the "wheat versus weeds" debate in any time or place can reveal a lot about the nature of the field in which both are growing.

"He put before them another parable: 'The kingdom of heaven may be compared to someone who sowed good seed in his field.'"

When it comes to the green and growing realm of sowers and seeds, of crops or gardens or common houseplants, I am admittedly inadequate, uninformed, even nonchalant. During all our years as property owners in spacious suburban tracts, I could never get too excited about the difference between crabgrass and Kentucky blue. That was not a popular position with my husband, neighbors, or the salespeople from lawn services who, for a price, would rid our portion of the creation of undesirables. My husband learned to take responsibility for my indifference, the neighbors trusted him to do so, and the lawn service people took their chemicals elsewhere.

But Jesus' insistence on the presence among us of a green and growing Kingdom, and the labors of a divine sower of gospel seed, has caused me to reconsider my greenophobia, to attend to my tendencies to plant abuse. Jesus and Matthew prod me to allow this alien spirituality to challenge my own wheat/weed equations.

In the realm of gardens and grain, as a grower and a sower, I am an abject failure. I don't even think to ask the theological question put by the slaves of the parable's master: "If you sowed only good seed, where did these weeds come from anyhow?" It all looks okay to me. And I am never tempted to yank anything out of our garden by its roots, for I know that I do not have the foggiest idea of its worth in the real gardener's scheme of things. I simply sit on my front porch on summer afternoons and graciously receive the unearned gratitude and compliments of passersby for the explosion of beauty in our yard, the beauty that is the result of another's efforts, vision, and skill.

All of that is sheer gift of the grower and sower in my house; his passion, delight, and energy evoke the beauty, and only my connectedness to him brings such beauty so close and present in my world. That truth allows me to enter the world of the parable, to face the mystery of seeds and sowers, good and bad, and to ponder my connectedness to the Master of all the world's fields.

If I were as good a Christian as I am bad a gardener, perhaps this parable would be less unsettling. The absence of anxiety and my confidence in another's care make for bad stewardship in one arena, but better theology in another. It is not even a tendency to spiritual or ecclesiastical weed-pulling that is my besetting sin. A young seminarian once touched her hearers with her pain, and that of many of us, with a hard truth. "I love this church," she said. "This church that I love is filled with people whose opinions I despise. But if they should leave, it will no longer be the church I love." She is very wise, but it is uncomfortable wisdom.

The sun might shine on the just and unjust, but I would prefer to apply a bit more fertilizer, water, and care to some parts of the crop that is springing up than to others. That is the dilemma for the larger church, and for this parish, not to mention for the planet itself. The vestry, the budget people, the clergy struggle with it in concrete ways: given finite resources, are there categories of humanity that deserve more of our fertilizer and care than others? And if so, who or what determines the identity of wheat and weeds? The in's and the out's, the good and the bad, the right and the wrong, the deserving and the undeserving: how is the faith community to tell who's who?

Beyond even the church's response in an often unfriendly culture, there is the sometimes literally burning issue of the purity of the church itself. Is the coming of the Kingdom dependent upon the purity of the church? Are the elect an elite? And what makes them so?

Jesus' parable, and Matthew's telling of it, offer no easy answers to the questions of good and evil, of salvation and judgment. A "God will get THEM in the end" self-righteousness—whoever "them" may be—has had devastating consequences for human beings with our propensities to get the jump on judgment. Some hard lessons of our history books serve as harsh reminders of human limitations. Jumping the judgment gun is dangerous business, dangerous to the souls and bodies of so many. The church has too often martyred its own, and others. The ashes of those accused and burned as heretics and witches soil our corporate soul. A propensity for purity has brought humanity such well-known institutions as the Inquisition, the Crusades, and an assortment of pogroms, civil wars, and well-policed ghettoes. We reap still a harvest of tears from a misplaced zeal for righteousness.

It is no accident that only Matthew's gospel gives us Jesus' parable of this mystery of wheat and weeds that are intertwined and indistinguishable. For his community was still a Jewish one, struggling to remain so in the face of their faith in Jesus and in the midst of a religious realm that had gone up for grabs with the destruction of the Temple that sat at Israel's heart. Matthew and his people found themselves accused as weeds in an ancient field, as they tried to make Judaism safe for newness and for Jesus. Matthew's community was desperately trying to hold it all together.

The witness of their experience of faith in this Jesus, crucified and risen, is still true for us all: passion, not purity, is the measure and ground of God's inclusivity. The call is to die for the sake of love, not to win for the sake of being right. In the end, Matthew failed to preserve a Jewish/Christian church. But he leaves us a gospel—with its challenge to stay open to God, and close to all that God is growing in the crowded field of creation.

The confusing field that was first-century Palestine yielded a rich crop anyway. A Gentile Christianity that connects the likes of most of us to the God and Father of our Lord Jesus Christ. And the richness of rabbinic Judaism with its profound claims of an ethical God and a divine Wisdom at work in history, and the witness of its awesome faith in its dangerous vocation as God's chosen people. It is tricky business, this mystery of good and evil, of suffering the presence of it all, of forgiving the confusion and the demands upon our patience and energies and resources, and foregoing a purity for the sake of a waiting upon the enigmatic sower who will gather his own harvest.

It requires some way of holding fast, staying rooted in God's goodness, rather than yielding to a fanaticism that destroys another. It means discerning the difference between a prophetic word and a judgmental one. And often the only way we can know that is through a sacrificial offering of ourselves, rather than making others the victims of our violence or apathy. It means preparing for a future that is God's by acts of commitment, rather than predicting a future for ourselves by acts of control. For church leaders and church people of many traditions, for those on opposing sides of ominous issues, it means staying, not leaving; it means embracing, not excommunicating.

The Good News is that the church is a parable itself of that mysterious ever-present Kingdom, a feisty field of goodness and badness, sown and presided over by a Master who has no interest in the purity of the green and growing crop, but a passion, delight, and energy for its coming to be.

It is our connectedness to the sower that matters, not the purity of the field. Ours is a God not much interested in purity. A God who has worked God's purposes in a drunken Noah, a murderous Moses, a much-married Solomon. A God who has sown himself into the human soil of our own flesh and blood through a family tree with the likes of a sleazy con artist like Jacob, an adulterous David, and a host of wicked royal progeny. And Jesus' grandmothers are every bit as questionable. Matthew lists Tamar the cult prostitute, Rahab the whore, Ruth the foreigner.

God's purity is as suspect as our own—and in that we might trust that the coming of God's kingdom is in no way dependent on the purity of God's church. We do not have to keep the church safe for Jesus. Thank God. Our fascination with the fate of the wicked weeds mirrors that of Jesus' disciples—in our fear of failure, and in our anxieties about our own weediness that make us ready to jump the judgment gun on others.

But the harvest belongs to its Lord. The destiny of the weeds will fuel fires, we are told. The good grain will be gathered into the owner's barn. All are embraced by the Lordship of a dying rising sower of seeds, and grower of grain—a Lord who knows first-hand the fate of grain. Grain is for breadmaking—the Bread of the Kingdom, a people blessed to be broken, shared, and consumed as He was, as He is still, the bread that nurtures and sustains this Body gathered; that we may continue as a living parable of God's mysterious, everpresent Kingdom. Bread to provide a foretaste of the harvest feast, the gift of the harvest's Lord, a gift of passion, delight, and energy to connect us with the One who makes the Kingdom present in the world.

C. The Preacher as Storyteller:
a sermon shaped by narrative

You couldn't have asked for a finer day.
The temperature was ideal for the end of May.
A few fleecy clouds dotted a bright blue sky.

The gently blowing breeze was just enough to keep folks from perspiring
    through the solemn outdoor graduation ceremony,
and not strong enough to blow the program pages back and forth,
    or to make sounds of static over the P.A. system.

The chairs had been arranged in neat rows across the lawn.
The entire area was bounded on three sides
    by the venerable buildings of the seminary cloister.

Overhead, a thick canopy of bright green leaves
  atop cathedral pillar-like oak and maple trees
    shielded the area from the glare of the sun.

The end of three long years of formal theological education.
For students, spouses, family, faculty, and friends
  it was clearly a moment for words fitly spoken—
    words to celebrate significant achievements,
    words to summarize a rich array of learning experiences,
    words to send graduates forth into the challenges of ordained ministry
      with confidence and courage.

Most of all, it was a time for words, nourished from the Scriptures,
  that would draw all our attentions to the Word of life—
    the One from whom the candidates had heard a call,
      and without whom neither the ceremony nor the seminary
      would have had any reason for being.

The Scriptures were read, the preacher rose to speak,
  the congregation leaned forward to listen.

The preacher was a bishop of the church,
  a widely published theologian with a strong reputation
    for a high view of Scripture
      and a vigorous commitment to the proclamation of the Gospel.

He began by decrying the moral state of contemporary culture,
  and the lack of a clear, uncompromising alternative evident in the church.

Warming to his theme, he expressed his outrage that a large eastern seminary
  had recently called a Unitarian as its new Academic Dean.

He challenged and exhorted the graduates to deploy themselves firmly
  against the advancing tide of secularism
    infiltrating orthodox Christian faith.

His zeal carried him through thirty minutes of variations on the theme.
Finally he finished and sat down.

The lessons of the day had never been mentioned.
The grace and power of God had been neither announced or invoked.
The indwelling presence of the risen Christ
  had never been brought to our attention.

But the urgency of defining and defending the boundaries
  of Christian doctrine and behavior—
    that had been propounded decisively.

Diplomas were distributed.
Eucharist was celebrated.
Everyone was dismissed.

You could see that some folks were highly pleased
  with the marching orders the preacher had issued.
"Powerful preaching!" they said with satisfaction.

I was empty, angry, and sick.
Taking time to calm myself, I approached the bishop.
Thanking him for coming to our campus, I told him quietly but candidly
  how disappointed I was that I had not heard the Scriptures preached
    or the gospel proclaimed.

He did not respond with rudeness or reactive anger.
He just looked at me, quizzically.
"Unless we take a stand for the Christian faith," he said,
  "the church may not survive!
Much of what passes for Christianity today is rank and outright heresy!"

Perhaps he is right. He is, after all, a bishop.
Guarding and defending the faith once delivered to the saints—
  that is a fundamental part of his job.

And yet, I'm not so sure—
At least I am not sure that his sermon was the best way to go about it.
"Do you want us to go and gather the weeds?" the servants asked the master
  in the parable of Jesus that Matthew tells.

"No," replies the owner of the field.
  "If you gather up the weeds right now,
    you will uproot the wheat as well."
It is easy to think, is it not, that health of the harvest
  is directly dependent upon the rigor of our weed hunts?

God knows how dearly I wanted to uproot that bishop!

In the Parable of the Sower,
  told a few lines earlier in Matthew's gospel,
    it surely looks—at least to the untrained eye—
    as though the sower doesn't care a bit
      whether anything grows in the fields at all.

In this parable,
  it looks as though the householder doesn't care enough about the crop
    to step in and separate the good stuff from the bad.

Both of these garden-growing strategies are utterly riddled with risk.

But on those strategies, apparently, for some mysterious reason,
  God has decided to bet the farm.

Questions for Reflection

Having listened to these different ways of proclaiming the word of the Lord in the Parable of the Wheat and the Tares, respond to the following questions.

1 Apart from your agreement or disagreement with their interpretations of Scripture, their particular focus, or their perceived degree of rhetorical polish, which sermon resonates in your ear most deeply? Which comes closest to the way you tend to preach?

2 If your normal mode is quite different from one or more of these, is that because of your clear preference? Or do you see patterns here that you wish you could follow?

3 Do you vary your preaching style under special circumstances? Under normal circumstances, to which type do you tend to return?

You might also consider the interrelation of the categories we are employing in this exploration. Your primary "preaching parents," for example, may have been very effective pulpit essayists, throwing in a story here or there to illustrate their points. By temperament and experience, however, you may be much more at home in painting verbal pictures with your sermons. From over your shoulder comes the question from your parent (perhaps not even reprovingly): "What is the point of your sermon?" Neither of you can find it. Your sermon, obviously, doesn't cut it, you conclude. Any sermon worth its salt has a clearly identifiable point. Then suddenly you remember the words of poet Archibald MacLeash: "A poem should not *mean,* but *be.*"

■ 7 ■

When Do I Resonate Most Clearly?

Theological Soundings to Which We Are Attuned

Up to this point, the emphasis has clearly been on the "your way" side of our title, *Your Way with God's Word*. We have been ruminating about who we are as persons, on the assumption that there is an intimate connection between "person" and "preacher." The question posed early on, however, now begins to assert itself with some urgency: are we focusing so much on the "personality" dimension of Phillips Brooks's dictum that we are losing touch with the "truth" dimension? Will the result of the journey we are taking leave us in a place where we will preach our own biographies—the very thing Brooks so explicitly warns us against?

It is not helpful to set up this problem as an either/or dichotomy: objective truth versus subjective experience. The so-called objective truth of which we often speak as Christians is a revelation from a personal God to persons—from Subject to subjects. The objective record of revelation in Scripture is an account of how subjects, as individuals and in communities, have received and responded to a self-disclosing God. Objective truth is always and inevitably an expression of "inter-subjectivity": persons communing with each other about their communion with God.

Yet the concern for objectivity is not misplaced. Individuals and groups of peoples have an inveterate tendency to create the world in their own image. This tendency was noted centuries ago by the Greek philosopher Xenophanes, who observed that people in every culture depict the gods as clones of themselves. Sarcastically, he went on to say that if horses, cows, pigs, and chickens could talk about how they understood deity, they would speak of the gods as horses, cows, pigs, and chickens. While impossible as an abstract ideal, the call for objectivity of truth is a reasonable call for a check and control on subjectivity as self-preoccupation.

So how do we get it? Where does it come from? The only reality check that we can run is an inter-subjective check. How does our experience of God look when we submit it in conversation with others in the religious community—both our more immediate communities, and wider cultural, geographic, and historical communities? My perspective can neither be proved nor summarily put down by sharing it with others. It can, in dialogue, however, be modified, redirected, and enriched.

This is a mysterious business. Not all points of agreement in the conversation are signals of truth; not all points of contention are signals of error. We do believe, as Christians, however, in an inter-subjective conversation process through which the Spirit of God "leads us into all truth." Preaching, in other words, is exploring, questioning, criticizing, learning, and reassessing while it is proclaiming. The question, then, can be reformulated: not as "How can I get back from 'personality' to 'truth'?" but rather as "How can I discern my preaching voice in conversation with the community?"

The faith community that comes to us through Scripture and Christian tradition provides the possibility not only of confirming or correcting our own ways of speaking, but also of resonating with them. By ourselves, our voice at times may have all the richness and power of a tin whistle. Brought into interaction with the voices of others to whom God has spoken, our voices may sound more like an organ—or may take on a role as a significant (though not solo) member of an orchestra.

Do you remember how lonely Elijah felt, after he had first stood down Ahab, Jezebel, and the four hundred prophets of Baal, and then fled for his life when word of his victory reached the ears of the queen? God took him on a rigorous retreat. At the end of his forty-day journey, he eventually heard the still small voice (or the sound of God's sheer silence). In that eerie "speech beneath speech," he heard something that was as heartening to him as it was surprising: he was not alone. There were in Israel seven thousand who had not bowed the knee to Baal. Having company helps.

What kind of company do you have? When are you among those with whom you deeply resonate? The "company of preachers" of which you are a part—what is it like? With whom do you find it easier to strike up a conversation about who God is, and how one goes about proclaiming the grace of God? With whom is it hard to carry on a conversation—either because you just can't make out what they are saying, or because, although they are saying it clearly enough, you profoundly disagree?

Let's wade into the middle of the conversation in the community of faith, searching now not so much for personal reference points as for theological points of orientation.

Characters, Models, Passages, and Principles: sacred stories that give our voices depth

The next series of questions provides a variety of ways for you to celebrate your particular resonance (or dissonance) with various voices in Christian tradition. Some of these potential points of contact are more likely to appeal to you than others, based on your homiletical parenting, your personal experiences, and your tendency to operate primarily as a poet, essayist, or storyteller. As before, spend time with the questions that seem to speak to you most directly.

---

1 With what biblical characters do you particularly identify? With whom do you have the most difficulty identifying? Who might be your preaching biblical patriarchs and matriarchs (even though they may have been bit players in the biblical drama)? In your preaching, are you a Dorcas, an Elizabeth, a Luke, a Jeremiah?

2 What are your favorite texts and books of Scripture? With which books do you resonate least clearly? What Scripture texts do you find it easy to preach? What texts do you find it hard to preach, whether you like them or not?

3 Which of the various Christian doctrines—incarnation, original sin, atonement, faith, grace, sacraments, mission, last things—are most important to you? Which are least important?

4 Who are significant figures for you in church history? With whom do you strongly identify? Which ones are embarrassments or sources of irritation?

5 What liturgical patterns do you embrace? What forms of worship do you find unhelpful or off-putting?

6 What forms of sacred music do you enjoy the most? the least?

7 What forms of Christian literature (doctrinal, devotional, moral, missiological) do you find particularly nourishing and insightful? Which ones do you find you just can't get into?

What are we listening for in all of the above? Persons, passages, and principles that you tend to preach *about,* of course, but, more significant, persons, passages, and principles that you preach *through.* These, for you, are entry points, windows on the word of God, compasses for your sermon journeys. They are not the notes your sermons keep playing, but the musical instruments with which you like to play them. Does your preaching sound like Daniel, or like Esther? Like Incarnation, like Sin and Judgment, like Law and Grace? Listen to your preaching. Preacher, what do you hear?

Don't be surprised if you find a theological depth and resonance that has been at work in you all along, and which you can now claim with greater intentionality and benefit in your preaching.

Roles, Concerns, Allegiances, and Entanglements: passions that give our voices focus

As a preacher you are doubtless an integral part of a particular religious community in a specific social setting. What are your activities and relationships? The answers to these questions will provide some indications of your preaching passions and gifts as well.

1 What tasks in church leadership (besides preaching) do you most enjoy? What tasks do you most dislike?

2 What kind of justice issues do you feel

■ the most energy around?

■ the most burden for?

■ the most hopeless about?

■ the least concern for?

3 What church programs energize you? enervate you?

4 What engages you most about the church beyond your own denomination?

5 What duties are you charged with by virtue of participating in the councils of your own denomination? What do you like best and least about being a denominational representative?

6 When you dream about the church as it ought to be, what visions come to your mind? When you consider the present state of the church, what is it that most makes you want to weep?

7 What kind of interest and energy do you have for dialogue with other Christian denominations? with other world religions? with the secular culture?

8 What do the words "pluralism" and "inclusivity" stir up within you?

9 If you ever gave up on the church, where would you go?

Two kinds of preachers tend to wear thin in a hurry: those who preach in intellectual or emotional abstractions, and those whose every sermon seems programmatic and agenda-driven. This is not a matter of being too comforting or too challenging. Sermons of comfort and challenge alike can be engaging or off-putting. The question, rather, is: Does the sermon somehow bring the real world into focus and bring a theological perspective to bear upon that world, so that we can see how God calls us to engage it?

To shift the metaphor, every sermon needs a heart. The questions in this chapter are a way of helping you to take the pulse of your ministry. What warms your heart? Makes it race? Causes it to skip a beat for terror or for sheer joy? How does that heart become the heart of the sermon?

■ 8 ■

With What May My Preaching Be Compared?

Free Associations That Suggest Distinctive Flavor

T he strategy will shift somewhat in this chapter. We will try to make some connections that may seem less obvious. Indeed, we will be taking some rather bold leaps, going on some pretty wild rides. In a word, this chapter is a sacred space for radical free association.

The imagination, as noted earlier, is often most insightful when it pulls together things that seem to have nothing in common. Seeing things in unfamiliar ways can be the source of unanticipated insight and explosive creativity. Sounds a bit scary, but what we are actually talking about is *fun*. In this chapter, we are invited into play—free play, opening ourselves to the insights about our preaching that might flow from some unexpected places.

Recently in a homiletics class we were talking about the subtle but marked differences in tone between the sermons of two preachers. We threw a number of high-sounding abstract phrases at the distinction, all academic, and all equally unsuccessful. Finally one of the students had an intuitive burst: "Both of these sermons were strong, clear, and sharp. But the first one sounded like a trumpet. The second sermon sounded more like a saxophone."

The comment described the difference precisely, and from that starting point we were able to spin off a number of ways in which each preacher offered the gospel with a particular flavoring. After all, one does not go about playing a trumpet in the same way one tackles music with a saxophone. Each of the preachers left the discussion with a clearer sense of his own instrument and of the techniques that would be most effective for tuning and playing it.

Another benefit from the discussion became evident when we realized how unproductive it would be to ask whether the trumpet or the saxophone was a "better" musical instrument. They are simply different. In some circumstances, one or the other might well be more fitting. But to ask which one of them made "real" music would be absurd. How much better for players of each instrument to focus on mastery of music for that instrument, rather than trying to compete, or to mimic their artistic counterparts!

---

1 Focus your attention for a moment not on your own preaching, but on the preaching venture more broadly. What is it like? What words, images, and stories spring spontaneously to your mind when you hear the word "preaching" or "sermon"?

2 Now be a bit more specific. Select one or two of the following, and write a few free-flowing paragraphs (without stopping to censor your spontaneous thoughts as you write), starting with this sentence: "Preaching is sort of like...."

- telling a story
- calling a square dance
- playing in a concert
- running a race
- selling a product
- giving birth to a child
- painting a picture
- writing a research paper
- making love
- fortune telling
- swimming
- stating a medical diagnosis
- acting in a play
- playing an active sport
- pleading a trial case
- writing a poem or a short story
- having an argument with a friend
- doing carpentry or plumbing
- being a parent or a friend
- juggling
- sailing
- raging, weeping, confessing, rejoicing
- serving as a manager, chief executive officer, or dean
- entertaining an audience as a stand-up comedian
- doing therapy or counseling (as therapist or patient)
- issuing orders to military subordinates
- farming or gardening

3 At this point you may well find that a host of other associations are jumping out and dancing. What are they? Give them some room to move.

4 Now come back to your own preaching and sit quietly beside it. Pick three of your sermons and ask them (yes, THEM) the following questions:

■ What color are you?

■ What musical instrument are you?

■ What fruit or vegetable are you? (Or what kind of casserole?)

■ What kind of game or sports activity are you?

■ What kind of dance are you?

■ What kind of outdoor places do you take everyone to?

■ What kind of building or automobile are you?

■ What kind of zoo animal are you? Farm animal?

■ If you were being touched by someone who is blind, what is your texture?

■ What kind of picture have you painted for us? (What kind of work of art do you happen to be?)

---

5 Now rate your preaching between
■ Rough and Smooth

■ Round and Square

■ Bright and Dark

■ Thick and Thin

■ Marching and Dancing

■ Running and Walking

■ Joking and Complaining

■ Working and Playing

These lists have doubtless generated a number of other possibilities for imagistic comparison. Follow through on some that seem promising. What catches the corner of your eye about your preaching in the wake of this flurry of free associations? Where might these insights take you, if you didn't scowl at them or scare them? Seasonings, spices, distinctive flavors do not make a meal, but they make a tremendous difference in whether or not the meal is appetizing.

■ 9 ■

Where Do I Feel Connected?

Preaching Experiences That Center Us

I t is time to come back down closer to earth after the soaring we have just been doing. The journey on which we are engaged is turning back in the direction of home. The hope is, of course, that home will look a bit better than it did before we went on vacation. These last two chapters in Part II will bring our attention back more explicitly to the preaching task itself. Even here, however, there are some ways of engaging the familiar territory that may help us to see it in fresh perspective.

Thus far, we have often resorted to imagery that is centered in the senses of sight and sound, with a scattered reference here and there to the sense of taste. Preaching can, I think, also be imagined in terms of its fragrances or aromas. If prayers can rise like incense, surely sermons can do so as well. It does not work particularly well, however, to pose the question: "How do your sermons smell?" (Trust me, I've tried it, though the embarrassed laughter that follows has set me to wondering why the seemingly neutral word "smell" carries more negative connotations than do the names of the other senses.)

There is another sense, however, that has not received much attention on this journey. That, of course, is the sense of *touch*. Our "feel" for things is often harder to put words around than is our experience of the other senses. It has to do with balance and bearings, with vague yet strong apprehensions concerning our sense of place: where we are comfortable, for whatever reason, and where we just don't fit. Where does your preaching "feel right"?—that is what we are about in this chapter.

"Good vibrations," obviously, are no guarantee that a preacher is exactly where she or he ought to be. But again, we are not at the moment trying to pass judgments, either positive or negative. The name of this game is description rather than prescription. We are trying as preachers to be attentive to what is in the *experience* of our preaching life, trying to be alert to what we are working with as a necessary prelude for deciding what we make of it.

So then, where and with whom do we feel connected as preachers? Where do we feel that we fit, that we are in rhythm or in sync? Having already taken some soundings in relation to *personal* and *theological* wellsprings, we will now try to ascertain some of our distinctive sources of *homiletical* inspiration.

Satisfactions, Challenges, Frustrations, and Favorite Spots: preaching places where we like to stand

How we stand in relation to our preaching experience is very important. How we feel about what we do depends a great deal upon our perceived success record—in spite of all we hear and tell ourselves about how "being faithful" is more important than "having something to show" for our preaching. Most of us feel more comfort or energy in some preaching situations than in others; we are not equally accomplished in our preaching across the board. That may tell us something about our preaching voices—not that we can or should at all costs avoid tight spots. Knowing where we like to preach can help us have a clear sense of the most stable centers from which we can launch out.

1 What have been your greatest joys and deepest disappointments in preaching?

2 Where have you sensed your greatest successes and failures in preaching? Describe in general terms the kinds of preaching that you most enjoy and most dislike.

3 What particular gifts for preaching do you believe that you bring to the task?

4 What gifts do you not have that you wish you had? What kinds of preaching skills are you not particularly interested in developing?

5 In what seasons of the church year do you like best to preach? Least? What special days (like Christmas, Pentecost) are particularly enjoyable or challenging? Why?

6 With what kinds of special occasion services (weddings, funerals, healing services) are you most comfortable? Least comfortable?

7 In your preaching, do you find yourself most frequently addressing issues of doctrine, moral responsibility, pastoral concern, spiritual deepening, church history and tradition, biblical teaching, or social analysis?

8 Do you find it daunting or delightful to preach with small children? adolescents? middle-aged persons? the elderly? folks of greater or lesser educational or economic opportunity?

9 Are you more comfortable preaching in congregations of greater or lesser racial, ethnic, and social diversity?

10 In what kind of preaching spaces do you feel most comfortable? Are you a pulpit preacher or an aisle preacher? A large-church or a small-church preacher (by choice or by necessity)? An "every Sunday in the same pulpit" preacher? An itinerant and/or occasional preacher?

11 Are there characteristic methods or patterns you employ in preparing to preach? Describe these in some detail.

12 Do you most regularly use notes, a manuscript, or no written text at all? If you vary delivery strategies, is there any pattern?

13 How do you assess the extent to which your sermons have been effective?

14 What steps do you take, regularly or occasionally, to enrich your resources for preaching? What kind of opportunities for continuing education do you take, or would you like to take if you could?

15 What very particular, specific goals do you have for the development of your preaching?

16 It is sometimes said that every preacher has only one sermon that is preached over and over in a variety of ways. What would that sermon be for you? To what central themes do you find yourself frequently returning in your preaching?

17 How, specifically, does your praying inform your preaching? Do you simply ask for divine guidance at the outset and at various points along the way? Do you imagine the biblical narrative or context? Do you enter wordless, centering prayer?

18 Does your praying in preparation for preaching usually take place alone? Do you pray with music or with quiet walks? In what specific ways do you experience your place for sermon preparation as a sacred space? Do you pray with others over your preaching?

You probably preach with some regularity in many of the places named in this section. That makes it all the more important for you to discern your particular homing instinct. We can operate with greater ease in unfamiliar or risky territory if we have a sense of where we are in relation to familiar country. What have you discovered by walking through this last set of questions about your preaching "comfort zones"—strong places that can serve for you as energizing points of departure when you are called into homiletical adventure, risk, and danger?

Siblings, Cousins, and Assorted Other Relations: preaching colleagues with whom we are in rhythm

Earlier we looked at the influence of your preaching parents and your preaching matriarchs and patriarchs in Scripture. You may also have identified some great-great-grandparents—persons in your denominational or worship traditions with whom you share a certain family resemblance. Now it is time to look around you, rather than backward in time. With whom do you *currently* share not only the preaching task, but also a similar vision for it and a similar way of coming at it?

Some of your contemporaries may be closely connected—preaching sisters and brothers. Others may be a bit older or more removed but still accessible—like uncles and aunts. Some may be more akin to cousins. Who are the folks around you now that you can talk to?

It goes almost without saying that "talk to" does not imply "always agree with." It is impossible to get a conversation going with some people because all they ever say is, "Yes, that's true, you're right!" There are many ways of disagreeing, however. There are some folks that you just can't wait to play verbal tennis with—it's more fun than practically anything else you do. There are some folks with whom disagreements are forever unproductive, and others with whom you don't even share enough common ground to fight on.

Your preaching colleagues are a potential treasure. Remember Elijah. If preaching is an ongoing conversation, you need to be, on a regular basis, with others whose business it is to be the facilitators of the preaching conversation.

On whom can you rely for mutual support in the preaching life? Select some of these questions as centering points for your reflection.

1 To what extent do you share your preaching experience—preparation, tapes or manuscripts, evaluations—with others who preach regularly?

2 How involved are those who hear you preach in your sermon preparation and evaluation?

3 Who are soul friends to you in the preaching journey? Do they more closely approximate siblings, cousins, or aunts and uncles?

4 What particular family resemblances do you have with preaching peers?

5 What kind of family fights are you privileged to engage in?

6 If you don't think you have much in the way of homiletical friends and family, who are the most likely prospects?

7 What qualities would you most value in a close preaching colleague? To what lengths are you willing to go in order to establish a working/playing relationship with a preaching colleague?

8 What skills, qualities, convictions, and experiences could you bring to a close collegial relationship—what some other lonely preacher would give anything to receive, and could not be purchased at any price?

9 In what particular ways might your preaching modify and develop over time if you were in an ongoing interchange with significant homiletical others?

More than in any other chapter, the questions here have some clear implications for immediate action. What kind of collegial cultivation on your part is invited—even required—as a faithful response to your preaching vocation? Perhaps it is possible for a period of time to survive as a preaching Lone Ranger, but it is not possible to thrive as one. Jesus sent his disciples out two by two. It is not good for preachers that they should be alone!

When God called Samuel, Eli did not tell the boy what God was saying; he helped Samuel to pay attention (even though the message was not one Eli wanted to hear). After Elizabeth named for Mary the Word conceived within her, Mary was released to sing *Magnificat*. Who can serve as an Eli or an Elizabeth for your preaching word?

Your homiletical home does not have to be restricted to a set of rhetorical, seasonal, or congregational coordinates. In fact, more important than any of these are the preaching folks with whom you feel both in tune and at home.

■ 10 ■

Why Do I Bother?

Preaching Visions We Want to Share

T he final chapter in Part II is the briefest, and in a way the most difficult. The question can be simply posed: "If one day you are gratefully recognized by someone as his or her preaching parent, what do you hope you will be remembered for?"

The question is asked not to round off the journey symmetrically, but to put it in terms of the inevitable, very personal impact of a preaching ministry. Why do we bother to preach? Yes, we preach because we think the gospel is important, and should be proclaimed to all nations. Left just like that, however, it is altogether too abstract.

Preaching, whether done well or poorly, is an ongoing conversation—whether fascinating, challenging, nurturing, confusing, abusive, or just deadly dull. But it is always person-to-person—an "inter-subjective" revelation. If you are not convinced of that, remind yourself of all the people who are angry or apathetic about the gospel primarily because of poor preaching.

I seriously doubt that some, or perhaps any of your preaching parents are aware of how profoundly they have affected your understanding of preaching and of the Good News. Life-changing sermons are often delivered whose preachers never know what they have set in motion. Since the full growth of seeds planted may not be evident for years, the garden may not even realize at the time what has been planted there. You will probably never know just who your preaching has influenced, and how. That is, for many reasons, a good thing. In the last analysis, while we broadcast the seed, we are not the seed itself, nor have we the means of ensuring the health and growth of what we send forth. The harvest belongs to God.

Too much of "how would I like to be remembered" is as self-serving as it is useless. Yet preaching models are important. The most important learning that any of us receive or foster is not information transfer or social conditioning—it is personal knowledge that comes only by way of interpersonal sharing. People took note of the disciples, the Scriptures say, because "they had been with Jesus," not because they had emerged from a training session clutching a spiffy new game plan for world transformation.

What, then, do you hope it has been like for people who have been with you as you have worked and played at proclaiming the gospel in the preaching conversation? There is not necessarily any inordinate self-preoccupation in that hope, nor is there any likelihood that you will be able to effect by your own power the kind of healthy influence that accords with your deepest hopes and ideals. After all, those whom you influence will need and want to develop their own distinctive preaching voices. They would, at best, be poor imitations of you. But they cannot develop their own preaching voices if no one takes the time and the intentional care to talk with them. How can they possibly find *their* way with God's word unless you share with them *your* way with God's word?

■ What distinctive qualities of your preaching do you hope will be remembered by others? What qualities do you hope will be helpful to them as they discover *their* way with God's word?

The Bureaucrat Whose Voice Was Welcome As It Was

A Homiletical Meditation on the Calling of Matthew

Matthew 9:9-13, Mark 2:13-17, Luke 5:27-32

When you come right down to it,
   what is there to say about Matthew?
Scripture gives us precious little to go on.

What are we supposed to make of Matthew?
The answer isn't obvious.

Flip through your mental file of sermons on St. Matthew.
I'll bet at least some,
   perhaps most, maybe even all those sermons
      fall into one of two categories:
        "Fill in the gaps" sermons, and
        "Glory in the gaps" sermons.

"Fill in the gaps" sermons go like this:
   "Now, the gospel doesn't tell us much about Matthew,
   But we do know that he was a tax collector,
     and from that we can safely infer A & B & C.
   When Jesus called him, Matthew left his tax collecting table and followed,
     which means he surely must have gone through E & F & G.
   You and I, like Matthew, are called to leave and follow,
     which means we must, we ought, we should do R & S & T.
   And God will honor our obedience
     by gracing our discipleship with X & Y & Z."

"Glory in the gaps" sermons are easier to outline:
 "Now, we don't know much about Matthew,
 But most folks don't know much about *us* either.
 Lack of renown didn't keep Jesus from calling Matthew,
 And low visibility doesn't keep Jesus from calling us.
 Thanks be to God, there is a place for Matthew, and for each of us,
  in that great and glorious company of Apostles Anonymous."

Don't get me wrong.
There is nothing heretical,
 or even homiletically improper
  in either of those sermon forms.
But I wonder if either is well suited
 to those of us who want to get a better sense
  of *how* God has called *us* to preach?

The "call" to preach can be persistent and pervasive,
 mysterious and elusive.
A preacher-in-the-making (and that is every one of us)
 can often be haunted,
  even bedeviled by a sense of "call."

"What does it mean to be called to preach?"
That isn't an abstract theological question
 we can leave somewhere on an out-of-the-way shelf.
It's a question that pricks and pulls at us—
 a question that never really goes away and leaves us alone.

Each of us does have a personal testimony—
 a story of one sort or another.
Each of us is familiar with the calls of apostles, prophets, and martyrs
 that punctuate the pages of Scripture.

Perhaps some of us can even articulate a "theology of preaching"
 with more or less precision and detail.

But regardless of all the resources at our disposal,
    questions about our call to preach
    keep on coming up for all of us:
    "What does 'my preaching ministry' *mean?*
      What does my calling to preach tell me about who I am?
        about where I have come from?
        about where God wants me to go?
        about how that is relevant when I stand up to preach?"

Do the gospel accounts describing Matthew's call address such questions?
Maybe, if we look hard enough.
No. Maybe, if we look *soft* enough—
    if we don't jump in to plug the awkward gaps too quickly.

"Follow me!"
"Matthew rose and followed," the first two gospels clearly tell us.
Luke's account is even more arresting:
    "He got up, left everything behind, and followed."

Tax collector one minute, disciple of Jesus the next.
 That's as dramatic and decisive a vocational turn-about
    as one could possibly imagine.

None of this "first let me go and bid farewell to my family" stuff.
No dickering, or dealing, or delaying tactics—
    "Yes, I'll be glad to consider working with you, Jesus,
      but first I'd have to liquidate my business and settle my affairs."

No talk about "transitioning";
Just action: bridge-burning action.

Matthew gets up and walks away—cold turkey.
To the tax table and all that goes with it, Matthew "just says no."

What a wonderful example of obedience and trust!
What an indictment upon those of us who hesitate, or speculate, or dawdle!
What an inspiration to those of us
    who have trouble making vocational transitions!

If Matthew can do it, by the grace of God, so can we!
Let us, like Matthew....

HOLD IT!!
WAIT A MINUTE!!
NOT SO FAST!!
TAKE ANOTHER LOOK AT THE TEXTS!!

Matthew *hasn't* cut himself off from all his previous associations.
Matthew has traded the tax table for the dinner table.
And will you look at the folks he's eating with?
   All his old cronies in that filthy business
     he supposedly has left behind.

So much for cold turkey transitions!
Matthew may have burned his bridges, but he hasn't sold his boat!

And that isn't all.
There are more than tax collectors at this party.
There are all sorts of other low-lifes too.

Analogous outcasts—other folks just as untouchable as tax collectors:
   ass drivers, camel drivers, sailors, and casters,
   herdsmen, shopkeepers, bloodletters, and butchers,
   tanners, bath attendants—
WHERE WILL ALL THIS END?

Maybe just where Jesus wants it to end,
   the frowns of Pharisees notwithstanding.

Whether we are lay ministers or clergy,
   we talk about conversion
     as a necessary part of our vocational formation.

And well we should.
We have no business preaching conversion
   if we are not ourselves converted.

Conversion is a process—
    a process of Damascus road epiphanies,
      and humdrum daily drills.

We hope and believe that, if we follow the call we hear as faithfully as we can,
    in time, the grace of God will bring us to a place
      that is very different, and much better,
        than the place in which we were
          when first we heard God's call.

Out of that, surely, we will one day be able to preach God's word
    with integrity and power.

It may be so.
God grant us all the grace of such conversions.
But some bridges need not, and should not be burned.

If God calls us, it isn't for our pedigree, our performance record,
    or even for our potential.
It's because God intends the family of faith to include
    an infinite variety of members,
      a family that wouldn't be complete without our particular brand
      of weirdness, warts, and woundedness.

It might just be that God is not as interested
    in our aptitude for theology, exegesis, preaching,
      liturgy, or pastoral care,
    as God is interested in—
      our unsavory associations.

Wouldn't that be disconcerting!

Unsavory associations.
The sort of folks who hang around the banquets
    that the gospel texts describe.

The sort of people Matthew ought to get some distance from
    if he's going to be a respectable disciple and a decent preacher.

The sort of people that law-honoring, God-fearing,
  self-respecting religious leaders
    wouldn't be caught within smelling distance of.

The sort of people that Jesus cares about so *profoundly,*
  it almost seems that he is concerned about their kind *exclusively:*
    "I have not come to call the respectable people, but the outcasts."

What if the main thing you and I have to offer God
  is a particular point of contact with a certain special outcast?

What if we need to be as sharply, fully formed preachers as we possibly can be,
  just because God thinks that *one special outcast*
    is worth all the effort in the world—
  and *we* are the ones, because of our unique experiences,
    who are particularly positioned to make the invitation?

What a tragedy it would be, if,
  in getting on with God's "program for our life,"
    we marked the stages of our growth as preachers
      with notches of homiletical respectability!

Can't you just envision us—an intrepid band of preaching disciples,
  armed with professional, state-of-the-art,
    exegetical, rhetorical buckets and brushes,
  saluting to the call of: "Follow me,"
  marching toward the outcasts of society, and
  scrubbing them raw with suds of respectability.

It's enough to make you giggle,
  if it weren't enough to make you weep.

What is clear in the accounts we read of the banquet at Matthew's house
  is that Matthew's friends are Jesus' friends—
    unsavory though they are.
And I acknowledge that I am filling in a gap here—
  but I wonder if part of what makes this party possible
    isn't a deep, unspoken hope-against-hope that tugs at every guest:

"Matthew is my kind of people. If Jesus will associate with Matthew,
   do you suppose that he might talk to me?"

If that is so, then—
   It's a good thing Matthew didn't burn all his bridges.
   It's a good thing Matthew didn't automatically decide
      that "tax collector" and "disciple of Jesus" were in every point at war.

For if Matthew had decided that,
   then Matthew might have silenced a significant part of his preaching voice
      in a desperate determination to follow his preaching vocation.

Does "Follow me" mean that I will have to give up some things?
Absolutely. No question about it.

But what, and how, and when, and where, and why—
   those are different questions altogether.
Questions we will need to wrestle with
   throughout a lifetime of discerning and developing a preaching voice.

What a pity if a misguided attempt to "follow the example of blessed Matthew"
      took us off on a wild goose chase,
   burning down bridges we should be maintaining,
   building up respectable homiletical castles—
      castles that, even as we build them,
         render us inaccessible—
            inaccessible to those for whom Christ gives his life,
            inaccessible to those whom Jesus wants to meet through us.

What a mercy that the banquet at Matthew's house
   invites us and requires us
      to come and sit at table
         with all the outcasts in every generation
            whom Jesus calls his friends!

Part III

Toward a Homiletical Spirituality

How Do You Convene a Sermon Conversation?

S o far, so good. Now what? What do you do with the insights of your personal discovery? How, as a preacher, do you engage in the sermon event as a full participant, without hogging the conversation? "Truth through personality"—how do you "fuse one to another," as Phillips Brooks envisioned, rather than merely tie them together?

There is one possible model that we can discard fairly quickly: the ranting and raving (or smooth soft-selling) television evangelist. "Pulpit personalities" they may be; preachers who convene a Christian community of continually deepening conversation they are *not*. This is not necessarily an indictment of their motives, but it does raise serious questions about the theological appropriateness of their methods. Whatever else it may mean to shape and share your preaching voice, taking center stage is not the "high calling" of God toward which you are pressing.

Is there a better model? Let's head for a place that is as unfamiliar to most religious traditions as it is an apparently unlikely source of homiletical insight: a gathering for worship by the Society of Friends.

There is deliberate, informed speaking in a Quaker meeting. No one is solely designated as the preacher and no one has prime responsibility for the outcome. At the meetinghouse of Friends, no sermon is ever "delivered," like a UPS package, but rather, *brought to birth* through the shared efforts of many participants who enter a very spacious conversation. Space is created by extended periods of silence. It is not dead silence but "full silence."

The Word of God, says Fred Craddock, "proceeds from silence." The richness of God's love can never be exhausted by any volume of words, or any artful combination of them. Words are always pointers beyond what they sound like to what they mean, which can never be enclosed by any definition of terms.

The Society of Friends keeps this deep theological truth at the heart and center of their worship. There is room for silence so that all may have access to Fullness. Individuals speak as they are moved to speak, and all are welcome to give voice to what, together, the community has been listening for. But no one looks for an opportunity to take the floor, nor does the floor belong to anyone, even the one who is speaking at the time. Eventually there emerges "a sense of the meeting," which is more than any one voice, and may well not be identical to what any individual has said. It is, in many ways at once, a fascinating vision of the ministry of preaching. But what does it offer for those of us who preach in a sermon setting that is more mainstream?

For a brief moment, set that question on the back burner, and focus again on one we asked in chapter 2: "What is the place of the preacher's voice in the conversation of the sermon?" This is not, we said there, a question that applies only to the preacher's voice; it can also be asked of all the other voices that we need to work into our sermons—the voices of Scripture, the congregation, the culture in which we are all immersed, and the liturgical patterns of our worship.

How does the process operate with respect to all these other voices? Let's come at that question by way of some bad examples. How do you respond when:

- a preacher calls your attention to all sorts of intricate bits of background biblical exegesis?
- a preacher goes on at length about "the liturgy which is particularly appointed for the celebration of the feast for which we gather here today"?
- the sermon is stacked with statistic upon statistic citing the rampant extent of poverty, hunger, or child abuse?

I'll bet you don't respond too kindly, although there may be a certain sense of ambivalence or guilt surrounding your frustration. After all, you tell yourself, this is surely important stuff. If the preacher didn't think it was relevant, it wouldn't have come up. Still, all this information turns the sermon into a research paper at best and a data-dumping ground at worst. This is not the Good News you came to church to hear. Even if you have heard a lot *about* the Good News, that is not the same as hearing it. "Maybe," you think, "it's my problem. I must just be resisting the gospel."

Probably not. The preacher is reporting, not preaching, putting forth "truth tidbits" (or even sizeable "truth chunks") as you observe from the sidelines. There is no sermon conversation going on here. This does not feel like a Quaker meeting, but a partisan political speech or a television talk show. There is no space for a "sense of the meeting" to emerge. The preacher picks up one or more of the voices, and "lays them on you." Even if those voices are artfully integrated, you are still left to overhear them. They aren't addressing you. Or, if they are, you are not being invited into the conversation as an active participant. God's Word is dispatched through (or is even identified with) the word from Scripture, perhaps in combination with the words from culture, congregation, and/or liturgy. The same conversation block occurs when the preacher prattles on about his or her "personal experience."

How can this be so? After all, the preacher is not being "objective" or "detached," but "personal." Data about oneself, however, even very intimate data, is not necessarily interpersonal communication. Indeed, the more intimate the details that are shared in a sermon setting, the more the congregation may be left at a distance. That may be because of a certain sense of embarrassment concerning self-disclosure which is inappropriate in a public setting. Or it may be because the experiences being shared are so far removed from the experiences of the listeners that what the preacher intends as a bridge between herself and her congregation is actually a gulf. I think, however, there is a deeper reason still.

Even if we are drawn into the preacher's story, just as in the case of sermons that deposit chunks of exegetical, liturgical, or sociological detail, we are not being drawn to the presence of Christ crucified and risen. The words of the sermon, however earnestly intended, are functioning as *idols* that obscure rather than as *icons* that mediate.

Let's get down to a couple of cases. I have in mind two preachers, each of whom I have heard on a number of occasions. The pattern is predictable. The first preacher never makes it more than halfway through the sermon without telling the congregation about some erudite piece of historical theology of which he is the proud possessor, or some important ecclesiastical responsibility that he is currently discharging. There is at best a tenuous connection between the experience he shares and whatever it is that the sermon is trying to say. The problem is obvious.

The case of the second preacher is more difficult to describe. She is very explicit about trying to find a point of contact between her world, the world of the Scripture text, and the world of the congregation to which she is preaching. Usually she begins with a "story," as she terms it. What that comes down to, however, is almost always this: "As I thought about the gospel lesson, it reminded me of something that happened to me last night," or "Last night I had experience X. Isn't that just like what we heard in the gospel lesson for today?"

What is the problem here? Her concern to make connections is valid and there is significant revelatory potential in her insights. But her sermon listeners are forever having to watch *her* as she looks at her own experience. Then they have to watch *her* as she looks at how her experience parallels something in Scripture. Then they have to watch *her* watching out for how there might be a parallel between *her* experience and what *they* experience. Long before the sermon is over, they are all "watched" out, and feeling left out as well.

Flannery O'Connor, the great Southern short story writer, in adapting an insight from novelist Henry James established a cardinal rule for those concerned with effective communication: "Show us. Don't tell us about it!" That rule applies full force to preachers who want to engage their listeners in the sermon conversation. As listeners, we must be brought in. We do not have to "talk back" in the sermon. It is perfectly all right for the preacher to say all the words of the sermon without any interrupting dialogue; but the speaking of the preacher must be shaped in such a way that our concerns are not just aimed at, but incorporated into the sermon conversation.

So the preacher must speak not just to us *about* God, but *with, among,* and *for* us to God. And any speaking *for* God *to* us that the preacher does must be deeply rooted in an understanding of Emmanuel, "God *with* us." This, of course, is what the Quaker meeting attempts to honor. If this principle can be embodied in the preaching process, the *I* of the preacher will not be distracting or intrusive. It will provide an *eye* through which the congregation can look at themselves, the world, and God, as John and Caroline Westerhoff made clear in their preaching conference titled "The 'I' and the 'Eye' of the Sermon." The *I* of the preacher's experience will be a window. It will be an *I* with which I can immediately identify, even though the particulars of the experience the preacher shares may be very different from my own.

Once again, how can these things be? What does a preacher do to make it happen? If the preacher *does not enter* the conversation, it is unlikely that the congregation will make connections with God's word. If the preacher *dominates* the conversation (however unintentionally), it is unlikely that the congregation will make connections with God's word. What do we do to make the connection more likely?

The simplest and perhaps most fundamental thing to say is that the preacher's personal experience needs to be wedded to an empathetic imagination. While I never know "just how you feel," since everyone's experience is to some extent unique, I can, without explicitly identifying my experience as my own, offer it as a vision for your consideration. I can try to describe the tones and textures of an experience to which I have paid attention in a way that will invite you to pay attention to your own.

Instead of saying "Look at me looking at my experience of the world," I can simply say "Oh, look!" and proceed to spread out a canvas. You are then free to explore, and to take or leave what you find. You are more likely by far to be captivated if you have the space to do your own looking, than if I am constantly in the picture, directing your attention to my act of pointing things out!

This may sound a bit tangled, so again, some examples. The "image" sermon on the wheat and the tares that you read in chapter 6 obviously grows out of the preacher's own experience. The camera's lens, however, moves from produce markets to weeds, to the preacher (cast simply as a "zealous gardener"), to God the householder, to the weeds and wheat that are growing side by side in all of us. While "I" occurs several times in the sermon, it is not attention-grabbing.

The "argument" sermon makes explicit use of personal experience as a lead-in illustration. That is only to focus our attention, however, on issues that operate in a much larger garden than the one in preacher's backyard.

My "story" sermon is essentially the recounting of a personal experience. "I" does not come in, however, until the climax of the action, and then that "I" is used primarily as the sermon's turning point. The hope is that listeners will first identify with my sense of righteous indignation and then go on to identify with the sense of being called to account by a God who, in judging fairly, will not abide judgmentalism.

The fruits of one's imagination can, through the use of images, arguments, and stories, be used to illuminate biblical stories, cultural situations, congregational dynamics, and liturgical principles. It can add a dimension of depth to them without shifting attention back and forth from the preacher to the issue, or simply dealing in details of personal biography. This is the kind of preaching that Phillips Brooks has in mind, I think, when he talks about fusing truth and personality in preaching, rather than simply tying them together.

I have, I believe, stood in the shoes of all the "voiceless ones" described early on in the "Zechariah" sermon that opened this book, but I do not need to tell you about my experiences of that. I can summarize the experience, not in an abstract statement, but in a clearly focused image that attempts to engage you, and to evoke a spark of recognition. Similarly, there is no question about the fact that the struggle for vocational identity unfolded in the "Matthew" sermon has been (and remains) central in my experience. How effective would it be, however, for me to begin the sermon with "I have a confession to make: I have had a long, hard struggle with what it means to be a preacher, and that struggle is very real for me—even as I speak to you today"?

There is no end to the ways in which you can use your own experience to make your preaching come to life and serve as a vital witness to the reality of the human condition and the grace of God. There is also no standard or formulaic way to do it. Your thoughts and feelings and struggles and insights can be incorporated into the characters that populate the stories in your sermon, or the stories that sometimes *are* your sermons. Images and thought processes that have come through attention to your personal experience can simply be presented at strategic points in the sermon. At other times, the insights you have gained will serve as the underlying "game plan" for the way in which the sermon unfolds, and will work much better if the attention of the congregation is not focused on that fact.

Oftentimes you will not be able to "deliver" the insights you have gained (unless you drop them off like the UPS driver). You may, however, come at things from the opposite direction. "What would it take," you might ask yourself, "for this group of people to discover for themselves, with the help of this text of Scripture, the truth that has been so important to me?" Now you may be able to uncover a sermon strategy which will, as it were, serve as midwife in the delivery of a "live birth"—an awareness in your listeners that comes first-hand from their own encounter with God.

This last suggestion leads us to a deeper realization. The developing of your preaching voice is intimately related to the sharpening of your ear for preaching. The result of all the "listening to yourself" that you did in Part II is as much a better hearing of the Scriptures and of other sermon voices as it is of hearing yourself. Listening, speaking, and knowing are all developed in a communal context. As I listen to others speak, I hear myself more clearly. The more I know of myself, the more I pick up on what is happening with others.

As this awareness develops, I will be able to identify more readily how my perspective is serving as a lens or filter through which the other voices in the sermon conversation are being perceived and expressed. I am much more likely to confuse my reading of someone else's views with what they are actually saying if I am oblivious to my own angle. This awareness, in turn, may help me recognize when my voice is being directly and appropriately challenged by the other voices I am hearing. Rather than making my preaching more captive to my own perspective, clearer self-perception can liberate my preaching from a bias that is unconscious.

It is, in other words, perfectly possible that the primary result of listening for your voice will be a better hearing of the Scriptures and the gospel. People may remark when they hear you preach: "That lesson on which you preached today never made much sense to me before. But now I think I understand, because it really came to life."

Who could ask for anything more? Preachers bear the burden of helping those with whom they preach to bear the Word of God—to incarnate God's loving presence in their own lives. They cannot do that effectively without knowing and unobtrusively communicating something of "what it is like." They won't do that effectively if they simply sit their listeners down and tell them, "This is what it was like when I went through it."

The best conversations, paradoxically, are ones in which the most stimulating participants are fully aware of themselves and of their role in the conversation, and, at the same time, utterly unself-conscious, not thinking of themselves at all. If, in the course of the verbal interplay, it becomes fitting to say: "my experience has been..." they will share it in a minute. On the other hand, they will spend no time whatsoever prowling about the conversation's outer edges, looking for the first opening through which they can burst with, "The way I see it is...."

We don't hold conversations in order to flatter ourselves—at least not very interesting conversations. We gather to talk about matters of substance and importance concerning which we have much to learn and about which we have much to contribute. And when the conversation ceases temporarily (really good conversations are always suspended, never shut down), we come away individually enriched and more deeply bonded to one another. Preaching is like that. And that is what we are working toward in the process of finding and forming our preaching voices.

◼ 12 ◼

Celebrating Your Way With God's Word

"Celebration" is an easily trivialized word. "Spirituality" has also become something of a buzzword in recent years. The meanings of both words, I think, can be enriched by seeing them in relation to each other. At the very least, one without the other is a pretty limited affair.

Celebrations that consist in no more than whoops and bashes don't get us very far. There is something at once unfulfilling and addicting about being a full-time professional "party animal." If you haven't got anything worth celebrating, after you have blown off some steam and shared a barrel of laughs, what's the point? Whatever we mean by "spirituality," celebrations—of whatever sort—seem to need it.

"Spirituality" devoid of celebration is equally deadly. It is unfortunate when the connotations of pain, suffering, self-denial, and utterly other-worldly piety are the only ones allowed to surround it. Spirituality has to do with the uplifting of all we are and have received as human beings so that it can be touched and multiplied for the glory of God, a good bit of which has to do with honoring and enhancing the lives of human beings who have been fashioned in the image of God.

Any genuine celebration is always an uplifting, which is not at all the same as "showing off." When you celebrate the birthday of a friend, you give thanks to and for that friend. You pay her special attention, but you do not (if you are wise) put her on a pedestal. A little concentrated expression of appreciation seldom hurts anyone, but it is probably just as well that birthdays come only once a year. You honor your friend for who she is and for what she contributes to your community. But it would be pretty silly, wouldn't it, to prolong the festivities to the point where she could no longer do the things among you that are such causes for celebration!

It is good to celebrate your preaching voice, to recognize it as a treasure trove of gifts given to you—which sets you free to share with others out of your abundance. If you don't value what God has given you, how will you possibly be able to offer that with any effectiveness to others? So by all means uplift with abandon your distinctive preaching voice. Delight in it every bit as much as if, from some unexpected place, you suddenly heard the sound of a voice so beautiful that it almost took your breath away.

To lift up your gifts for preaching, however, is not simply to hold them above your head like a trophy being paraded by a champion before a wildly applauding crowd. To lift up your preaching gifts is to offer them in God's direction (which, is, of course, to offer them outward as much as it is to offer them upward). That, it seems to me, is the bottom line of any homiletical spirituality.

It is important in this connection to observe that "offering them back to God" does not mean that God simply teases us by demanding back with one hand what God has previously given with the other. No, think of conversation again. The giving and receiving of words in community is not simply an economy in which everyone endlessly passes coins around a circle, or where some people invest coins for the sake of luring everyone else's coins into their own pockets. Good conversation is a game in which the more freely you share—not pieces of your mind but portions of your heart—the richer you become. Conversation, in short, is not a "zero sum game." No one needs to lose; each and all can win without limit. God is always in conversation with us. Preaching the gospel, in fact, has the shape of conversation because it moves in rhythm with the dynamic of God's love.

The point of these brief reflections on homiletical spirituality is to say that careful attention to finding and forming your preaching voice is a central act of what, in Romans 12, St. Paul calls "intelligent worship": "I urge you," he says, "to present your bodies as a living sacrifice." Your preaching voice is not just a single element of that sacrifice, but a central focus. Turned in upon itself, homiletical self-perception becomes a hollow echo chamber. Turned outward and upward, it becomes a participation in the cosmic dance of grace.

Can we be more specific, more down-to-earth as to how this celebration of homiletical spirituality works itself out in the ongoing process of a preaching life? I believe we can.

Your preaching voice will in certain respects be different from the voice of any other. There are nuances of God's grace that you will be able to name and share in ways that are unique to your experience. That, after all, is part of why you are called to preach. You need to tend with care the gifts you have been given. If you don't share them, nobody will.

On the other hand, to turn your place in the choir of preachers into a primadona solo slot is something else again. Your distinctive voice gives you no grounds for carving out a particular piece of homiletical "turf" or for designating yourself the sole certified professional in a homiletical sub-specialty, and charging your clients accordingly. What you are seeking to hone in on and celebrate is a center, a place of balance, a place in which you have a clear sense of your homiletical bearings. From this center, you can and should reach out in all directions, stretching your limits as the preaching situation demands. We will best be able to extend ourselves as preachers, however, if we have developed a clear and well-practiced sense of where our center of strength is—which is not always synonymous with our "comfort zone."

An image from vocal music may be helpful here. A singer's voice has a *tessitura*, a set of notes that are at the center of a singer's vocal range. All singers regularly go both above and below their tessitura. There is significant overlap between the vocal ranges of sopranos and altos; in fact, for professional singers, there are several designated gradations on the spectrum between the highest and the lowest female vocal ranges, just as there are in the male vocal ranges. (And there is also significant overlap between the lower female and the higher male ranges.)

While a lyric soprano and a coloratura soprano can sing many of the same songs, there are some songs that are simply better suited to one voice or the other. Even if both sopranos sing the same song, their different vocal qualities are such that the song will sound quite different depending upon who sings it. Each voice can be celebrated.

An occasional return to questions that help you compare your preaching voice with other voices can be quite instructive. Different homiletical fruits, dances, musical instruments, and so on do not need to battle it out for "king of the homiletical mountain." The energy is better spent discerning the differences, developing the distinctions, and celebrating them all.

Interesting though it may be, however, the potential variety of preaching voices is not of value simply as an end in itself. There is no particular virtue, as far as I can see, in having a museum with a thousand varieties of homiletical voices all carefully tagged and neatly on display. There is need for a variety of voices, because there are a variety of ears who need to hear the gospel, and a wide range of situations to which the gospel needs to be specifically and sharply addressed. As preachers of the gospel we are all called to let God's freedom song ring out as far and wide as we can, "in season and out of season." Yet no one of us can reach everybody, everywhere, all the time, with equal effectiveness.

Once again, preaching is an open-ended conversation. There is no conversation artist so brilliant that he or she can speak for everyone.

Entertainment often takes place in theaters and night clubs. The houselights go down, so as to direct the attention of all the spectators to the songs and dances of those whose actions are spotlighted on the stage. Celebrations, however, have no need or use for spotlights; celebrations are community affairs. Preaching is not entertainment; it is a celebration.

How are you to get on with the celebration of your preaching voice?

■ Rejoice in your gifts.

■ Return, again and again, to your center.

■ Extend your range, as the occasion presents itself and the need arises.

■ Stay in conversations with as many voices as possible, to enrich the resonance of your own.

■ Keep in mind, and hold in your heart, that preaching is an ongoing conversation in which you are privileged to have a share throughout your ministry of proclamation.

Finding Voices for a Freedom Song

A Homiletical Meditation on
the Calling of Two Women Named "Mary"

Luke 1:26-55, 8:1-2, 24:10-11; John 20:1-18

"Let it be unto me according to your word."

"I have seen the Lord!"

It might be a good idea for preachers
    to post those phrases prominently in their pulpits—
        for, surely, on those two statements
            hang all that is of homiletical importance.

"Let it be unto me according to your word!"—
    radical openness to the grace God offers.

"I have seen the Lord!"—
    radical obedience to the risen Christ.

Receiving the Word,
    recounting the Word—
        that's what preaching is.

"Let it be!"
"I have seen!"
Both of these fundamental proclamations are uttered by women.
Whoever said that women couldn't preach!

Mary Magdalene and Mary, the mother of Jesus—
    what would *their* preaching voices sound like?

Chances are, we'd have to listen for them closely.
In the chorus of tenor and bass voices by which they are surrounded,
    it might be hard to catch those higher, softer voices.

"Let it be unto me according to your word!"
That's what Mary of Nazareth says.
But is that really *Mary's* voice?

What viable alternatives did Mary have?
What were her options?

The angel Gabriel was sent from God—
    and what did the angel come with?
        An offer?
        A request?
        A plea?

Doesn't sound much like any of the above:
    "You *will* conceive," the angel says.
    "You *will* bear a son."
    "You *will* call him Jesus."

But then, this probably was not the first time
    that Mary had been told what she would do.

Obligations issued by hierarchies—
    that's what set the tempo of the drum to which Mary marched.
        Hierarchies upon hierarchies,
        all of which she was expected to obey:
            —family hierarchies
            —tribal hierarchies
            —alien political hierarchies
            —ecclesiastical hierarchies.

Mary knew the drill.
Mary was well trained.

"Let it be unto me according to your word."
    What response could be more natural?
    What other response was even possible?

How can anybody swim against the force of an onrushing tide?

"Let it be unto me according to your word."
You were expecting Mary to say something else?

Throughout his gospel, Luke makes it clear he knows quite well
    the conditions and conditioners
        that have a grip on Mary's world.

Luke's gospel is alert to the position and the plight
    of those who are caught on the downside
        of social, sexual, political, and ecclesiastical systems.
Luke is keenly aware of what both Marys are up against.

Observe his sharp political eye; listen to his keen literary ear,
    as Luke describes the impact of Mary Magdalene's voice,
        when she tells the male disciples that the tomb of Jesus is empty:

    "Now it was Mary Magdalene, Joanna, Mary the mother of James,
        and the other women with them who told this to the apostles.
    But these words seemed to them an idle tale,
        and they did not believe them."

Why not?
Maybe it was because the menfolk knew that out of Mary Magdalene
    Jesus had cast seven demons.
Mary Magdalene had a history of listening to,
    no, being driven by voices that couldn't be trusted.

"'The tomb is empty'?—
    that woman is crazy!"

But maybe the common knowledge of Mary Magdalene's tortured history
    was simply an excuse.

After all, both Marys had something in common beyond their name.
Both of them were women.
Why would anyone in ancient Palestine pay any attention
    to the voice of a woman?

So how then do you account for the fact that,
    two thousand years later,
        the voices of *both* Marys are still ringing loud and clear?

Perhaps it is because God has a thing
    about silencing voices that are making too much noise,
        and magnifying voices that don't seem to matter.

"The Holy Spirit will come upon you,"
    the angel said to the maiden of Nazareth,
        "and the power of the Most High will overshadow you."

Did you get that?
    Overshadow—not overpower.
    There *is* a difference.
    It's the difference between invading someone, and inviting her.

"Greetings, favored one! The Lord is with you!"

Did you get that?
    Not a hit on Mary.
    Not a proposition or a bribe.
    Not even a moral evaluation stamped A+.

    Just a simple assertion of God's loving attention,
        an announcement of God's intimate, but non-intrusive presence.

That's not the way power operates in Mary's world.
No wonder Mary is "much perplexed" by the angel's words,
    "and ponders what sort of greeting this might be."

But it doesn't take her long
    to recognize real power, graceful power, when she sees it:

"Yes, Sovereign One," she says.
"I will sing your freedom song.
  I will carry the Holy Child.
  I will undertake the sorrow and suffering that this entails.
  Let it be unto me according to your word!"

"Woman, why are you weeping?" says the supposed gardener
  to Mary Magdalene, wracked with grief.
"Woman, why are you weeping?
  Whom are you seeking?"

"Sir," she sobs, "if you have carried him away,
  tell me where you have laid him
    and I will take him away.
  This is not just one more victim of Roman persecution.
    This is my Lord.
  What has already happened is an outrage.
  There was nothing I could do about it.
  But I will not just stand by helplessly
    if you have desecrated his body."

"Mary!"
"Rabbouni!"

"I am with you. Do not fear.
You need not cling.
Go—go and tell my brothers I am risen."

Did you get that?
The risen Christ is appointing Mary Magdalene
  to go and sing God's freedom song.
Even though she is a woman.
Perhaps *because* she is a woman.

After all, she is the one who, while searching for his body,
  referred to Jesus as *"my* Lord."
That personal reference, apparently,
  is not a matter of sentimental insignificance.

At least not to the author of John's gospel.
For John has Jesus say to Mary Magdalene:
    "Tell the men that I am ascending to *my* Father and *your* Father,
    To *my* God and *your* God."

Could there be a degree of personal intimacy with God
    that the voice of Mary Magdalene
      is particularly well suited to convey?

Yes, I know.
She *has* been bedeviled by seven voices that are not her own.

But for all I know, that may give her special insight
    as to how to talk with other folks
      who hear destructive voices in *their* heads.

This may all be speculation.
What is clear in the texts of Luke and of John
    is that two women are called to bear the Word.

And because they both agreed to sing God's freedom song,
    you and I are able to follow along
      in a graceful procession of preachers—
    a procession that stretches out
      across the entire sanctuary of history.

You see, God did not just up and decide
    to give a preaching voice to the voiceless ones
      on the day when the angel Gabriel was sent by God
        to a town in Galilee called Nazareth.

And the virgin Mary didn't just make up her freedom song
    right there on the spot.

As Luke, the storyteller, shrewdly recognizes,
    there are subtle, graceful, underground agents in Mary's life.
They are unobtrusive, but they labor—lovingly and powerfully—
    to liberate Mary from the bondage of her conditions and her conditioners.

Mary of Nazareth has preaching relatives.

Elizabeth.
The biological relationship between Mary and Elizabeth is not clear,
    but their homiletical relationship is surely evident.
Elizabeth is Mary's wise older sister—
    herself beset by the same conditions Mary is,
    but similarly graced by God as well.

Elizabeth does not know "just how Mary feels,"
    but she's got a good idea.
To her Mary comes in haste.

Mary's own revelation has been powerful enough.
Why does she have to go see Elizabeth?
Isn't God's own word sufficient?

Well, all I can say is that Gabriel put her up to it;
    and I'd just as soon not argue with an angel.
In fact, if I may be so bold,
    I think what Gabriel suggests to Mary makes a lot of sense.

Mary has heard God's word.
But how does she know that any human being can hear *her?*
Elizabeth does—she sees and says what Mary knows,
    before Mary has even said a word.
And that releases Mary's voice.

In Luke's exquisite theological artistry,
    while Mary receives and responds to the Word
        in the presence of Gabriel,
        it is only after Elizabeth's discerning celebration
            that Mary herself begins to sing:
            "My soul proclaims the greatness of the Lord:
            My spirit rejoices in God my savior!"

But, powerful enough though it is already,
    there is still more of God's energy at work here.

In Elizabeth, Mary has a preaching sister.
But she also has a preaching grandmother—
    Great-great-grandmother Hannah.

"My heart exults in the Lord," Hannah had sung in thanksgiving
    many generations before, when God released her
      from social disgrace by giving her a son named Samuel.

"My heart exults in the Lord!
There is no Holy One like the Lord.
The Lord is a God of knowledge,
    and by him actions are weighed.
The bows of the mighty are broken,
    but the feeble gird on strength."

Mary's song is sung
    in dancing interplay with the song of Hannah.

"Let it be unto me according to your word!"
    says Mary of Nazareth.
"I have seen the Lord,"
    Mary Magdalene proclaims.
For each of us, proclaiming the gospel is just as simple,
    and just as difficult as that.

Just as *difficult*—
    because it will not do for you and me
      simply to stand up and parrot God's freedom song.

The deepest truths of the gospel are always mocked by cheap clichés—
    counterfeits of a genuine preaching conversation.
Learning to listen for and to speak God's word is difficult at best.
Often it's excruciating.

Becoming a responsible participant
    in the preaching conversation is costly.
It will take everything we've got.

But preaching the gospel is as *simple* as
    "I have seen!" and
    "Let it be!"
For you and I do not carry the preaching conversation
    solely on our own shoulders.

We are surrounded by a great cloud of witnesses
    to God's power and mercy.
We have seen the Lord.
We have been overshadowed.
The Lord is with us.

That will be sufficient to sustain us
    in the sacred conversation.